Marriage

A COVENANT
OF SEASONS

MARY VAN BALEN HOLT

LIGUORI
PUBLICATIONS

**ONE LIGUORI DRIVE
LIGUORI, MO 63057-9999
(314) 464-2500**

ISBN 0-89243-537-2
Library of Congress Catalog Card Number: 93-77227

Copyright © 1993, Mary van Balen Holt
Printed in the United States of America

Cover and interior art by Laurie Shore Van Balen
Interior design by Pam Hummelsheim

This work is dedicated to

Joseph and Geneva Van Balen, my parents,
in honor of their fiftieth wedding anniversary.
They gave me my first experience of what
a Christian marriage can be. They continue to be
a source of inspiration to all who know them.

Rick, my husband, with whom I share the journey
and celebrate the seasons.
He is my resting place and my blessing.

Joshua, Emily, and Kathryn, our children.
They continually open new worlds for me.
They are God's gift to us.

TABLE OF CONTENTS

ACKNOWLEDGMENTS

This book has grown out of the experiences of many people. It is an effort to present a true picture of married life with its joys and sorrows, struggles and triumphs. It is an attempt to share the promise that the covenant holds—for the couple as well as the world.

I extend a sincere thank-you to all the couples who generously shared their stories with me and now allow me to share those stories with you. Some filled out questionnaires or wrote letters, while others shared conversations over the phone, around the table, and in quiet corners where we could spend some moments together.

Sharing our stories supports and encourages those of us called to journey through life with a partner. It also gives us a chance to reflect on the riches and opportunities that grace marriage.

I am deeply grateful for the honesty and candor of those who opened their lives to me. In an effort to maintain anonymity, I have changed many names and other identifying details. In some instances, the quotes are not verbatim but are a rephrasing of what was shared. Some examples are a combination of a number of stories. All accounts are based on true experiences of couples striving to be faithful to the vocation of married life.

I am especially grateful to my sisters, Elizabeth Delphia and Janet Distelzweig, who were only a phone call away day or night. Their experience and wisdom were invariably helpful. Their husbands, Michael and Howard, also were willing to share their thoughts and experiences.

The love and support of my entire family have always been a source of strength, and this project benefited from them as well. My brothers and their wives, Joe and Margaret Van Balen and Tom and Laurie Van Balen, have been abundantly generous with their time and hospitality. Laurie, the illustrator, spent much time making her artwork reflect the tone of the book. The contributions of my parents are too numerous to list; watching the children for us while I worked on the book was a tremendous form of support.

My husband, Rick, and our children have also been a great support, doing extra chores, giving me time alone to work, and believing in me and my efforts. Many times, as we have journeyed together for seventeen years, I have been blessed with Rick's willingness to share his spirit with me and to spend the hours together in prayer and conversation that help strengthen our love. I would also like to mention Father Gil Genest, whose faith and friendship has meant so much to us.

Much thanks goes to Kass Dotterweich, my editor. With insightful suggestions, she guided me through the process of writing this book. Her unflagging encouragement and enthusiasm for the project helped me continue when the task seemed overwhelming.

INTRODUCTION

$\mathcal{R}$esponding to any vocation, to God's call, is a bit like choosing one path among many at the edge of a meadow. Many may seem inviting, but one makes a stronger claim on our hearts. One captures our imagination and says "Come, walk my way" so convincingly that we say "Yes" to that path and "No" to the others. That is not to say that the others are less beautiful, more or less challenging, or less fulfilling. Rather, our reason for choosing a particular direction is often known by God alone: God, speaking powerfully to our soul.

And so, we choose. God calls us, and we begin our journey down the path that will give shape and definition to the rest of our lives.

This book is a reflection of the path walked by those who choose marriage: the journey to God with a partner. The vocation of marriage is truly our way to holiness. For some of us, this seems an impossibility. After all, marriage and family draw us into the world, into busyness. Don't these things distract us from God? Don't they focus our attentions on things of this world rather than on pursuing spiritual heights?

Marriage is, indeed, a calling that draws us into the very center of society and humankind. First comes the primary relationship and all that implies: getting to know each other, learning to live together, securing jobs that enable us to set up a home and put food on the table, learning to sexually express love and commitment to each other. Then, when children arrive, we are drawn further into the world. There are endless doctor appointments for infants and toddlers and never-ending activities with friends, school, and other interests that demand the support of parents. Children quickly plunge the family into the culture of the day.

How can all these demands of marriage possibly constitute a journey to God? Surely such a flurry of activity is not for those of us who are serious about a spiritual life.

Actually, immersing ourselves in the world within the context of marriage is an opportunity for us to encounter God and to let God touch the world through us. In the midst of it all, a sacramental marriage is the still point. It is the common center of faith from which we journey through confusing times, allowing us to travel about the world without getting lost in it. The path of marriage is not only the place from which we encounter the world; it is also the place to which we return for rest, healing, and renewal.

As I write, I am aware of the idealistic picture this paints. When we are experiencing a harsher season of our relationship, a winter or the pruning of spring, marriage may seem like the problem, not the place of healing or rest. It may be the place where we suffer great hurt. After all, where we are the most honest, open, and trusting is also where we are the most vulnerable.

But seasons come and go. The pain of springtime pruning and the cold loneliness of winter lead to renewed and deepened life. As two individuals sharing a covenant with each other and God, we can have faith even in difficult times. We believe that our marriage, with Jesus as a partner, is the reality that gives us the power to persevere, to be in the world and yet not be defeated by it.

Thus, marriage is not only the way to holiness for us but a sign of hope for the world as well. In cooperation with the sacred, we allow Jesus to touch and redeem the world through us. Our marriage is not only for the two of us who have committed ourselves to journey together toward God. It is for all God's people.

After living the sacrament of matrimony for seventeen years, Rick and I know that we do not travel our path alone. Jesus is very much with us. From the beginning, we knew it was the "three of us," and it continues to be so today. We have met the Lord in places we never dreamed of: at two a.m. feedings, in difficult work situations, in school problems, in intimate exchanges, and in conflict.

Like all vocations, marriage is filled with opportunities for prayer and spiritual growth. The difficulty is in recognizing these opportunities. They seldom appear in expected places; they seldom look like the stereotyped images of prayer and disciplines we have of those in "religious life."

Instead of giving what we earn to a religious order, we use our resources to support the lives of children born to us; we financially support the causes we choose. We relinquish claim to personal time and space, learning to be present and available to others with whom we live: spouse and children. We are drawn through them to become involved in the lives of others in the work of our community and the world. All are ways to serve and to love.

Of course, the call of marriage, like any vocation, has its dangers; getting sidetracked is easy. Ah, to get a good night's sleep, to hold on to the paycheck for personal use, to take off at a whim without accounting to anyone, to take care of our own emotional and physical needs without having to consider the emotional and physical needs of others. Oh, yes, the call of the culture to follow a self-centered way of life is strong indeed.

Fortunately, we do not face these challenges alone. Together with Jesus, we draw strength from our covenant, our chosen vocation, and the grace that is ours as a result of that choice. We travel together to God, touching the world as we go.

Like everything in life, marriage has its seasons. Nothing stays the same as it matures and develops. The seed falls to earth and is embraced in the quiet, dark soil. With time, it opens into a small plant that pushes through the soil's embrace to reach for the sun. It grows and becomes strong, providing cool shade, succulent fruit, and secure environments for God's nesting creatures. Flowers sprout and bloom and fade. Then, after gestating through the natural cycle of winter, they sprout again.

There is wisdom in seasons. Once children learn that the catkin will appear, fuzzy and silver every spring, that flowers return and trees grow new leaves, they do not mourn the part of the cycle that means "death." Autumn and winter become times to enjoy. Rather than grieving the lost green leaves of summer, children delight in the pile of gold and yellow ones in the fall. Not afraid that the warm breeze of spring will never blow across their cheeks again, children glide down snowy hills with glee.

Seasons, coming and going and coming again, teach us trust. We strive to live each season to its fullness. We learn to uncover and cherish the treasures each has to offer, letting go of one, knowing others will follow.

Marriage is a covenant of seasons. It means birth and beginning; it means death and loss. Marriage is filled with busy years and times of rest, times of working diligently to sustain the relationship and times to enjoy the fruits of that labor. Marriage is filled with the mystery of Jesus' own death and resurrection. As a partner in the covenant, Jesus promises new, more vibrant life. To those willing to embrace the winters and the dying, Jesus promises spring and resurrection.

The seasons of marriage, however, do not come once and then disappear forever; they come again and again. As we walk our chosen path, we walk through endless seasons. In times of darkness and difficulty, we remember the sunshine of spring; we trust both the current darkness and the light to come. In times of celebration and plenty, we give thanks; in times of hardship, we again give thanks. We are encouraged and nourished. Through the seasons, Jesus gives us a glimpse of the happiness and fulfillment of the life to come.

In marriage, we walk together: a threesome. We enjoy the seasons as they come and go and take from each what it has to offer. We marvel at the garden of life as it changes with the elements. We travel as a threesome, sharing the bond of a sacred covenant.

Spring

Walking down the hill to feed our rabbit, my feet sink slightly as the ground shifts under my weight. The earth, thawing from the winter freeze, sends its sweet combination of smells through the air. Birds nesting in the old honeysuckle bush sing—real songs, not winter calls alerting fellow feeders that food has been found. The spring songs that rise from the joy of knowing life, roused from deep winter sleep, is on the verge of bursting forth again.

Spring! Crocuses, red-winged blackbirds, leaf buds swelling and dusting the jumbled branches of the woods with green. Spring is a time of anticipating what is almost here. Beginnings are everywhere. Promise and hope are alive in every tree and bush, in every heart weary of winter's heavy wrap.

Spring is a time of dreaming big. Anything is possible; everything looms ahead. Gardeners see row upon weedless row of plants and bountiful harvests with every seed they drop into the earth. Children see swimsuits and lightning bugs, beaches and no school, the first time they play outside without a coat.

This, too, is the spring of marriage: full of excitement and dreams. Spring is a time of hope for the relationship, for it's ability to mature further in fidelity and faith. When a spring comes to a marriage, it brings enthusiasm and joy.

For the young couple, spring means feeling indomitable. They are special and unique. There are no communication problems, no incompatibility problems. Life unfolds, warm and full of adventure and joy.

For those married longer—those who have tasted both joy and disillusionment—spring means a breath of fresh air. Spring is a second (or third or fourth...) beginning. It brings renewed hope and trust in the relationship, in each other, and in God with them. The sense of being indomitable returns, tempered with the maturity of perseverance and the acceptance of God's grace. Perhaps for these couples, spring is even sweeter.

Spring is a time to relax in each other's arms, to share love, and to celebrate the rebirth of a relationship. Spring in marriage brings renewed hope, anticipation, and enthusiasm for the journey.

COMMUNICATION

A married couple experiences many springs as they go through life together. Their first spring is when their interest in each other takes root, grows, and becomes serious. For many couples, this season takes them by surprise, catching them off guard and sweeping them along.

"Please don't move to Cleveland!" one young man pleaded with his roommate, who was considering a job offer. "I feel like my relationship with Judith is a snowball rolling down a hill. Who will I talk to for some perspective? I don't think I want to get serious, but I can't resist it. If you leave, I'm a goner!"

The roommate left and, sure enough, after a few months the young man and Judith were happily engaged. The couple laugh as they tell the story. Spring is a time of intensity!

Like the gardener who rushes to turn the soil once it begins to thaw, a couple experiencing spring is eager to immerse themselves in each other, relishing the joy they feel in each other's company.

NEVER ENOUGH TIME

In the springs of a relationship, there is never enough time to be together, never enough time to say all that needs to be said. Even for those of us who have experienced many springs, the intensity of these seasons is difficult to comprehend. Why would anyone write a letter every day to the same person? How can there always be so much to say to each other? How can the two spend hours on the phone—often long distance—sometimes not saying a thing?

A single woman once complained that she felt neglected and left out when her companions began to date their future spouses. "How can they be so unfeeling?" she would moan. "The amount of time they spend with each other is ridiculous!" A few years later, when she became engaged, she confided to me that some of her single friends were resentful of her new relationship. "They just don't understand," she said.

I looked at her, smiled, and reminded her of our conversation years ago. She grinned sheepishly. "You're right. I guess you have to be there!"

How true. For those who have never known the splendid thrill of spring, no amount of explaining will help. For those who have enjoyed such seasons with the one they love, no explanation is necessary. The tremendous desire to be with the other, to share anything and everything—all the time—is overwhelming.

Most married couples relate favorite stories of the "early days" when they spent hour upon hour getting to know each other. Some who were separated wrote long letters. One woman remembers finding a huge postcard during a stopover in New York's La Guardia airport. She filled every inch of the card with thoughts and news to the man she would later marry. They had met only a few months earlier, and love had never been mentioned, let alone marriage. But they had spent many days and nights sharing their philosophies, hopes, and dreams. A spring was just beginning.

For some, their memories are of long walks or talks that lasted into the night and ended up in a restaurant over breakfast. One couple met at an island camp where they were both counselors. Eighteen years later, they can still hear the waves breaking and feel the cool breeze from across the lake.

The setting doesn't matter, and the topic can be anything: a good book, hopes for the future, favorite music, family backgrounds, jobs. Springtime communication is the sharing of two human lives: histories, presents, futures. The more the two learn about each other, the more they want to know.

SPRING AGAIN AND AGAIN

Fortunately, the new life of spring is not limited to your courtship, engagement, and the first few years of your marriage. Springs come to the covenant of marriage again and again.

"I find myself thinking about Ed off and on all day," shares a wife of fifteen years, a gentle smile dancing in her eyes. "We've rediscovered each other after a long period of being too busy with everything else. It seems silly, I guess, but I put notes in his lunches, he calls me from work, and we look forward to late evenings when the children are in bed and we can be alone together."

Another wife pinpoints little pockets of spring scattered through the years. "Sometimes after we've come through a time when we didn't feel close, I find myself more interested than usual in my husband's thoughts and feelings. No matter what it is, I enjoy learning more about him. People are so complex. We can never really know all about anyone, even our spouse."

People change; relationships change. Springtime is the season when you, as a couple, become aware of change and newness. You spend hours talking and rediscovering each other—even after years of marriage. Someone who loved hiking and exploring the outdoors at age twenty may develop asthma and a dependence on air conditioning at forty. A small-town girl is exposed to big-city ballet and develops a love for dance and classical music. A city boy whose closest encounter with a cow was the milk carton in the refrigerator becomes an old hand at milking and an enthusiastic member of the local dairy association. Someone discovers a talent for acting in community theater. Another finds himself struggling to respond to a growing sensitivity to God's call to serve the poor while remaining faithful to his commitment to spouse and children. These changes call on your faith in the covenant. They challenge you to let go of fear and open the relationship to grace and growth.

A springtime experience of getting to know your spouse does not always last for months, weeks, days, or even hours. Sometimes it is as brief as a warm breeze that blows unexpectedly into the cold of winter. In a moment, a sudden insight into the heart of your spouse deepens your understanding and ability to love.

"Springtimes to me are also realizations," says one woman married seventeen years. She remembers feeling resentful, sometimes lonely, because her husband spent so much time in his garden.

"One afternoon, we sat down in the grass next to a row of tomato plants he'd just put in. He started talking about the soil, how the plants would grow, and how he'd tend to them in the weeks ahead. I suddenly realized how relaxing and satisfying his garden time is for him. It's his relaxation, his quiet time. The garden is a place where he can just *be*." A brief moment of springtime put this wife in touch with a dimension of her lover and life partner that she had failed to grasp. "I smile to myself and feel a surge of love for this man I discover again and again through the years."

THE CHALLENGE OF SPRING

Learning to accept and encourage emerging facets of a partner's personality is the unending challenge of spring. Couples who have been married for thirty years or more develop new mutual interests after their children are grown and have left home. Others take courses together at local colleges, travel, or begin serious volunteer work. New worlds open and the new life of spring blossoms forth. They share their experiences, and their marriage is enriched.

Part of the joy and demands of the springtime season is to explore these changes whenever they come. One woman married two years shares her enthusiasm for a springtime moment: "I get excited about something or my self-esteem is in good shape, and I just love to share that with John. I feel confident that he's genuinely interested and happy for me."

You want to be together in spring, whether married for thirty years or engaged for a few months. This desire to spend time together is a bit like spring fever. When the first warm breezes blow, marking the end of winter, you want to be outdoors. You look out the window and daydream. You lay on a grassy hill, play golf, bike—anything to be outside. You anticipate the enjoyable pursuits of summer.

ngtime in marriage has the same effect. You get
    up in the intense feelings of being "in love." You want
to enjoy those times and dream about the life you're building
together or the one you'll soon begin. To an outsider, you
may actually appear foolish. You seem to "waste" so much
time. Ah, but that is the great gift of the season: "wasting"
time together.

"I brought home a briefcase full of work on Friday night,"
says one husband, "but after the jobs around the house were
done on Saturday, Andrea and I took a walk and talked about
nothing in particular. Monday came and the work was still in
my briefcase, but Andrea and I felt happy and close." Their
weekend had been blessed with a springtime.

SPRING PLANNING

Communication during spring seasons is often about plans:
plans for weddings, for a family, for a job, for a new home.
The gardener has a plan when the seeds are dropped into the
soil: beans on one side, tomatoes on the other, flowers all
around. Plans can change. If the plants do not flourish one
year, the gardener tries them somewhere else the next—
starting once again with a plan.

In the early days, a couple's life stretches ahead of them;
they spend a great deal of time talking and dreaming. As
married life goes on, spring-like planning and communication
centers on other, more specific endeavors. "I don't know
when we've ever had such an enjoyable vacation," shares a
woman married almost fifty years. She and her husband had
spent days poring over maps and planning their long drive to
Colorado. "We might just go again next year," she says with
a playful smile. "You never know!"

Whether planning or "wasting time," earnest sharing is bound to uncover differences. Every person is unique and brings a lifetime of experiences to the relationship. One couple shares this story from their early courtship days.

"We were out for an afternoon drive, and Joe suggested we stop to get something to eat. I was starved and thought that was a great idea. A few minutes later, we pulled into a grocery store parking lot. Joe's idea of a bite to eat when out for a drive was a loaf of bread and a package of cold cuts; my idea was a restaurant. When I expressed surprise and disappointment, Joe said, 'Well, if you're going to hang around me, you'll just have to get used to the way I do things.' Needless to say, we had an important conversation right there in the parking lot and cleared some things up right away!"

Part of the planning that springtime communicators focus on is the harvest to come; it must be manageable. Like a gardener who is carried away with the excitement of the season and "overplants," springtime communicators may inadvertently share more than they realize. Summer will mean an overabundant crop, and harvesting will be taxing. Earnest lovers know that time is their greatest gift; they relish it, anticipating a lifetime together.

Springtime communication is marked by a lack of self-centeredness; you focus on each other. With mutual enthusiasm and respect, you listen to each other and share yourself in return. You enter each other's world and share your own.

When springtime lovers listen, they do not look for error in an argument; they do not mentally assess possible gains and losses. Rather, they listen to each other because they are invested in each other's lives. She listens because what her spouse is saying will help her know him better. He listens because he wants to be open and receive whatever she is willing to give.

WHERE IS THE SEASON?

Springtime communication happens whenever there is an exchange between lovers that is freeing and full of hope. It may be a brief phone call or a long evening of intense sharing. Springtime communication is any moment that reflects God's desire to be one with us. God listens to us and holds whatever we entrust to him: our brokenness, our sin, our hopes, our fears, our joys, and our dreams. This liberating communication is one way you become a means for each other to encounter God.

One couple shares their enjoyment of rediscovering each other after coming through a particularly difficult time of distance and estrangement.

"We spent hours talking after the children were in bed. That meant late nights and dragging fatigue through the next day. But it was worth it. After months of thinking that we didn't really love each other anymore, we were surprised to find out how wrong we were. All kinds of false assumptions had blocked our communication. We were judgmental and quick to find fault. When we felt the real concern of the other and realized we were being heard and not just listened to, communication began to flow. We took time to be with each other, watched late movies, took walks after dinner, and re-discovered that we really did like being together. We felt free to be ourselves because we were so positive with each other."

When you empty yourself of self, the two of you as lovers allow God to penetrate your relationship. The unconditional acceptance you experience as you listen to each other mirrors God's love and enthusiasm for you. Your ability to become engrossed with each other mirrors God's insatiable desire to be one with you. Through communication in the springtime of a marriage, God deepens your commitment and creates the desire to share on more and deeper levels.

FAMILY

*T*he prospect of watching the plants grow fills garden-ers with anticipation. During spring, every day brings change: sprouts push through the soil, string-marked rows fill with green leaves, and tiny blossoms appear. Enthusiasm for the work ahead is fueled by images of a good harvest and memories of sweet produce.

A couple's experience of children and family life in the season of spring embraces an anticipation of good things. "The obvious springs are the pregnancies," shares one mother of three. "The promise of new life and the certainty of irrevocable upheaval in the family!"

Waiting for the arrival of a child is certainly a springtime in a couple's life. Whether waiting for the birth of their biological child or making preparations for an adopted child, the time is full of dreaming and planning. "What will he or she look like? Who will this child grow to become? How can we best love this child?" These are only a few questions all parents ponder as they lay side by side in bed, waiting.

Spring seasons are a time of openness to growth and change for the couple, and pregnancy reminds them of the mystery of life and the need for an unconditional acceptance of the unknown.

The time a couple waits to adopt a child is also filled with such wonderings. Those who choose to adopt an older child or a child with physical or mental disabilities demonstrate a special willingness to embrace life and all its unknowns. Their commitment is a sign of faith in God's sustaining presence with them and in the sacredness of all life.

"When we adopted our son," one couple says, "we knew he had some emotional and learning disabilities, but we felt we could offer him a stable home, love, and opportunities. He has also been a gift to us, bringing us closer together as we deal with the challenges. We have grown in our trust of God to be with all our family as we face the future. Our son has been a source of joy. He reminds us to appreciate simple pleasures of life, to let go of worry, and to take time to be together."

THE TWO BECOME MORE

The arrival of a child changes you forever. You are no longer "two," you are a "family." One father experienced the movement from "two" to "family" in a single moment: "Our marriage had a whole new connotation right at the moment of conception!"

Remembering the sleepless nights and the exhaustion, one mother laughs. "How do people find the time to conceive more than one child? I was always so tired, and the baby's sleeping habits were so unpredictable. When my husband and I finally tumbled into bed, all we wanted to do was sleep!"

A college professor confided that he and his wife had spent a sleepless night wondering what their son would choose to do on prom night. "Would he come home or go to an all-night party? He wore us out physically when he was young," he says. "And that was okay; we were young, too, and could handle it. Now, he's older and we're older—and he wears us out emotionally." Then the professor smiles. "He came home, by the way."

Whether a child's arrival means fixing up a nursery or cleaning out a corner of an already crowded bedroom, it always means lifelong changes for the couple.

Having experienced a long winter in their married life, one couple shared their struggle to rebuild their marriage through counseling and much prayer. During those months, they conceived a child. "The birth of our child was something to look forward to, a sign that our relationship had a future, that we were, in fact, moving forward together. His birth was a sign of great hope, a warm breeze blowing into the end of a winter chill."

One couple married thirty-five years cited the births of their children, their children's marriages, the births of their grandchildren, and family gatherings as continual sources of joy in their life together. They experienced springtime again and again, year after year, in one way or another.

AND A LITTLE CHILD SHALL LEAD THEM

Children are their own persons. Certainly, the environment you provide—emotional, spiritual, and physical—has much to do with how your children grow and develop. But your children are first God's children. God has blessed each of them with unique personalities and gifts. One of the joys of parenting, one of the springtimes with children, is being open to enjoy their uniqueness, to learn from them as they learn from you.

A quiet, intellectual couple is baffled by the social athlete their son is. Another man, who spent hours hitting a ball against a barn in the country and dreamed of playing baseball, is surprised by his son's natural aptitude for science and electronics.

"My husband and I have become lacrosse fans," chuckles one mother. "We had never seen the game before our son joined his school team. Now, a Saturday at the field is a pleasant afternoon for all of us."

I am reminded of the spring my husband gave me a packet of seeds labeled "wildflowers." I prepared the ground, planted the seeds, and waited. Weeks passed and nothing sprouted. Finally, plants that looked like possible flowers appeared. When they bloomed, all were yellow and orange. Then I noticed a bud on a low-growing plant and assumed it was some kind of weed. A week later, however, the bud opened into a lovely blue blossom—the only blue blossom in the garden. It was small but lovely and a welcome contrast to all the yellow and orange.

Children can be like that packet of seeds. You need patience, attentiveness, and the will to nurture—but you never know how your children will grow. You do know that each will bring a special color and form to your family and the world.

One retired couple, open to the surprises and turns life presents them, broadened their interests and experiences by remaining involved. The wife learned to enjoy a good basketball game, to manipulate Game Boy Tetris™ shapes, and to ride South Carolina's waves onto the beach. In return, she shared her love of reading, introducing her grandchildren to historical classics and new releases.

Her husband shared his knowledge of mechanics and engineering with the grandchildren and, in turn, learned more about electronics, dinosaurs, piloting a small plane, and cooking imaginary strudel on a cardboard stove. After he suffered a heart attack, the couple hesitated to travel. Encouraged by their son and reassured by their doctor, however, they resumed visits to "the kids" and continue to know the ever-blossoming joys of spring. "You gotta be with the kids," he says. "They keep you young. They keep you going."

Spring renews our hope and afflicts young and old alike with restlessness and the desire to get out and do something. Children do that to your marriage. They infect you with their own enthusiasms and windows on the world.

"We will never look at the night sky in quite the same way since we learned about black holes, the space/time continuum, and dark matter," says a young mother. "Our minds have been opened a bit wider and our reverence and awe of the Creator deepened by our children and their friends sharing these interests with us."

A part of the world and it's culture was broken open for one couple by their teenager's year as an exchange student in Thailand. Their son's experiences brought the Far East right to their own home. As a result, subsequent events in China, as the students struggled for democracy, were even more poignant for them.

New perspectives need not be so intellectual or complicated. A bean seed sprouting is exciting to every young child, and nothing tastes as good to them as something they grew themselves. Enjoying a fireworks display, the first taste of salty ocean water, or the beauty of a black cat moving stealthily across white snow are all experiences that children bring alive for a couple who has seen them a hundred times and have forgotten to look. In these moments, spring pushes through the soil.

One couple has become more interested in art and more knowledgeable about the Impressionists since their daughter discovered a doll and a book about her and Monet's garden.

"One morning she woke me up to watch a sunrise with her," the mother explains. "Sunsets are more suited to my biological clock, but I got up anyway. Wrapped in blankets, we sat on the front porch. Suddenly, the first stroke of reddish-orange appeared. I was amazed at how quickly it spread across the entire sky. I couldn't remember the last time I had watched a sunrise. It was beautiful. 'I wonder how Monet got all those colors,' my daughter puzzled out loud. I didn't know, but I walked around for the rest of the day marveling that such beautiful moments happen every morn-ing, that God has created such a world, and that I don't even notice most of the time!" Now members of the local art gallery, this woman and her husband spend a lot of time marveling at the talents of the masters. A spring for them dawned with their child's invitation to a sunrise.

HOPE NESTLES IN SPRING

Some of the sweetest springtimes children bring are those that follow the harsh elements of a long winter. In those moments, hope emerges.

How wonderful for a couple to carry on an adult conversa-tion with the child who, a few years before, thought they had nothing of value to say. What resurrection is experienced in the embrace of a father and a son who parted with harsh words years ago.

Charlene relates a problem with her teenage daughter. "She was on the phone constantly, her grades were falling, and she was moody so much of the time. Then, one night she announced that she'd be in her room studying, and if anyone called, she'd call them back later. To top it off, she asked me to help her with her social-studies homework. I looked at my husband and heaved a sigh of relief." Such a spring, when it breaks through unexpectedly, reminds us that seasons come and seasons go. The teenage years are part of a marriage for only a short time.

Respite from family growing pains is not the only thing that constitutes a springtime in your relationship as parents. Some of the simplest accomplishments in life bring a spring-time-like gladness to your commitment. Helping your child adjust to a changed routine, watching your child make a new friend, or cheering for your youngster from the bleachers (win or lose) are the daily moments of spring that often get lost in the shuffle of major events.

Granted, the peace found on the other side of a crisis involving a child is also a springtime relief. "My wife and I could spend time thinking and talking about other things for a change. The stress was gone. Everything seemed better," shares a husband. Enjoying the absence of worry, the sense of accomplishment, or a renewed self-esteem is like breathing sweet air that hints of summer and good times to come. Suddenly, the next trial is a challenge that can be met and mastered by the two of you; it no longer looms out there as an obstacle.

Parents of nine remember when three of their children faced life-threatening conditions—at the same time. Two were in automobile accidents and one was seriously ill. Prayer and pulling together got the couple through those dark times.

"We look back and see that God brought out a lot of good

between us as a couple during that time." Hours of physical care and support by family and friends, rooms filled with greetings, and the love that deepened and drew their family even closer together were all springtime moments that rekindled the couple's marriage. That period of time was a major spring that produced life in many ways for years to come.

WHERE IS THE SEASON?

Spring in a couple's life is especially poignant when they watch their children take faith into the world. The couple knows that their love for each other has fashioned the world for the better in some small way through the contributions their children will make. Children bring hope with their belief that they can overcome whatever difficulties they meet: personal as well as global. Children rekindle in their parents hope and enthusiasm for the future.

"When our son helped start a recycling program at his school, we became recommitted to doing more ourselves," shares one mother. "I was a sixties environmentalist, but time, family, and life's concerns dulled my interest. Our son's involvement made us take another look at what we could do together to be more environmentally responsible."

Today's world is full of grave problems, and children are aware of them: pollution, wars, armament buildups, drugs, crime, disease. After watching a television special on global warming and the world of the future, a ten-year-old girl shook her head and said, "If that's how the world is gonna be, we have problems! How come nobody's doing anything about it now?"

Your children's challenges are your challenges. The response of children to the predicaments of the world is varied. Some become depressed, feeling powerless. Most, however, find ways to hope; older children may even decide to take action, to confront the situations.

Children's efforts in schools and communities across the country are signs of their desire to make the world a better place. Their cries to the world are springtimes for you, cries to all of us to cling to hope, to look toward the future. Young people call us to a springtime renewal. Volunteering in programs like Habitat for Humanity and local church outreach projects can be experiences that rejuvenate your relationship, giving you a sense of community as a couple and as a family.

So many couples ache for this sense of meaning. They want to know the experience of faith and hope. Children, with their visions of peaceful and healthy coexistence, summon their parents to a renewed commitment—in themselves and in the world. The children will not sit by and let the world fall apart in their generation.

Oren Lyons, faith-keeper of the Onondaga Nation, speaks of the responsibility we all have to the environment and to the generations to come. He says that to us, the elders, the situation may look hopeless. But ask the youth, and they will say that it is bad but not impossible, not too late.

It is this gift of hope that children give their parents, this gift of faith that reminds them of God's saving love. Renewal is possible: renewal of a relationship as well as the world. Faith and hope, manifested in your children, will open your eyes to the signs of spring that exist in the world of your living room and in the larger world where greed and sinfulness maintain a desperate grip.

INTIMACY

*J*ust as the force of nature seems completely focused on bringing forth new life each spring, the relationship of a couple experiencing a spring season propels them toward intimacy. Their overwhelming desire is to be with each other and to share their thoughts, feelings, and physical selves. This is as true for a long-married couple rediscovering each other as it is for the newly in-love couple who spends hours gazing into each other's eyes. Intimacy, in all its manifestations, is the absorbing focus of a spring-like season.

Our culture is preoccupied with the material and physical aspects of life. Without reservation, it uses any means to appeal to the consumer with "intimate" overtones. It glorifies that which is shallow: physical beauty, extravagant possessions, and flashy occupations. Physical intimacy is separated from spiritual and emotional intimacy and is often reduced to satisfying sexual appetites. Little regard is given to the value of a permanent relationship. Commitment is dismissed as an infringement on an individual's freedom to "be himself or herself," a sentence to boredom and mediocrity for all time to come. Rather than a broad understanding that includes the intense sharing of what belongs to our deepest nature, an understanding of "intimacy" is limited to genital contact.

Actually, the opposite is true: only within a lifelong relationship will a couple find the freedom they seek. Far from destroying the individual, a permanent marital relationship offers the stable framework within which two people dare to uncover their true selves to find a meaning that grows out of their lives together. A lifelong commitment offers a couple the opportunity and freedom to explore and develop all aspects of intimacy. Knowing that they don't have to "get it right" the first time and all the time gives a couple permission to change, explore, risk, and make mistakes. When intimacy is not as successful as they'd hope, the couple has the time—and the long-range committed purpose—to try again.

"Sharing deep feelings with Leroy is not always easy," admits Stella. "He often interprets it as a request for help, and his response is to tell me how to 'fix the problem.' What I really want is for him to hold me, to listen to me, and to know me better. There are times when I get so frustrated that I think about never sharing anything meaningful with him again. But I do try again because it's important to us both. When we finally do connect, I feel more loved than ever, and we are closer because of it."

Part of the excitement of springtime in a relationship is the shared desire to know and be known. Both partners are eager to give themselves and to receive the other. The hours of sharing rekindle friendship and deepen spiritual, emotional, and physical intimacy.

COMING HOME

Springtime lovers experience a great desire to share sexual intimacy. Their desire for each other transcends physical attraction and becomes the natural consequence of the intimacy they share on other levels. The joy and satisfaction of sexual intercourse becomes an expression of intimacy that grows from early, sometimes awkward, expressions to more comfortable and fulfilling experiences. Integrating intimacy at all levels is the only way the couple learns to hold and love each other's spirit as well as body.

One couple shares a story of an early experience of intimacy in their relationship. They had known each other for only a few months but had spent much time together. "We talked about everything: our work, growing up, God, the desire to live a simple lifestyle, embracing values other than those of middle-class suburbia, how to plant tulip bulbs. Mainly, we talked about how neither one of us wanted to get serious!"

When their relationship was only a few months old, the young woman decided to tour Europe for the summer. The morning she left, the two took a few minutes for themselves, away from the bustle of family and friends at the airport. They went to a park, and the woman gave her friend a small gift she had made.

"When he put his arms around me and kissed me and held me close, I had the most overpowering feeling of coming home. I remember thinking how foolish I was to be going three thousand miles away when I had at last found a person who could hold my whole being—and who wanted to!"

The young woman went to Europe but wondered throughout the summer what this new relationship would mean in her life. The two had tasted intimacy. They had given themselves unreservedly to each other and had found the gift received and held. They both knew that whatever happened, their relationship would be a special one.

The sense of "coming home" that the young woman experienced is very much the essence of intimacy. None of our earthly homes is perfect. But in the experience of intimacy, the image of "home" is broader than a family home. Home is a place where you belong, where you go out from and where you return to. Home is a place where you can be yourself and be received. It is a place where you are in harmony with the surroundings. In religious songs and writings, "going home" often refers to final unity with God after death.

All these nuances of meaning describe some aspect of a couple's intimacy. Whether it is discovering the person with whom you can be "at home," as in the case of the young couple, or a husband and wife of many years comfortably reviewing their day's routine, the experience is one of intimacy.

Joseph Campbell, the late mythologist, speaks of finding the right person to marry. In his imagery, he refers to the two members of a truly married couple as the two halves of a whole that existed from all eternity and was split on earth. Marriage is reuniting that which once was one. In marrying, the two people give themselves to the relationship, which is their true identity. For Campbell, the union is primarily spiritual. Physical union is only the expression of the spiritual unity that already exists.

This imagery presents a longing for oneness, for completeness. Saint Paul presents a similar image when he speaks of all creation groaning toward unity with God. Our spiritual journey is one of discovering the union with the Maker of all that is. In a covenantal marriage, the husband and wife are joined and become a new creation. They do not lose themselves in the other; rather, they find their true identity, their full selves. Together, they journey to union with God.

SPRINGTIME SPONTANEITY

Intimacy strives for oneness on all levels. In the springtime of relationships, this oneness is spontaneous and effortless. Everything fits together. It arrives like the springs of nature. Flowers appear overnight where snow and dead leaves once covered the ground. Trees bud and leaves unfurl, responding to the warmth of the sun and the surge of life-giving sap that rises from deep within their roots.

In a relationship, the couple responds to the warmth and life-giving acceptance of each other's love. They share freely with each other. The experience of becoming vulnerable, becoming more deeply and completely known, accepted, and loved is the essence of intimacy.

A couple of seventeen years shared this story. One evening, all the frustrations at work along with the demands of being a wife and mother had become too much. Cindy, fighting tears, walked out of the house. She took a brisk walk around the neighborhood, letting her emotions surface while trying to figure out what to do next. A major work-related project was causing her a great deal of pressure.

"I was angry," she said, "at my family, myself, and at God for the way my life seemed to be going. After I had been gone awhile, Dan found me, and we walked together in silence. He slipped his arm around me and said that he believed in me."

Encouraged by Dan's confidence, Cindy talked about work and home and her frustrations at trying to juggle both. Dan listened, and they continued to walk hand in hand.

"After letting my frustration and anger pour out, I felt strengthened by Dan's support. I was finally able to say what was really worrying me: I was afraid. What if I failed with the project at work? I had put so much time and energy, so much of myself, into that project. I wasn't sure I could finish it, but I wasn't comfortable with the thought of failure, either. Dan didn't have any easy answers, but he told me he loved me no matter how things turned out. 'You are not what you do,' he said.

"I knew he meant it. As we walked home, I felt how deep and solid our love is. I began to think about getting the children to bed so we could enjoy a night together."

WHERE IS THE SEASON?

Times for intimacy are difficult to find, especially while the children are young. Difficult, however, does not mean impossible. You cannot afford not to set aside your personal and intimate time.

"Our occasional getaways as a twosome are most definitely springtimes at their very best," shares a young wife. "We choose a quiet, out-of-the-way place where we can be alone and close to nature. We hike and talk and travel the blue highways that the children will never sit still for. Best of all, there is time for intimacy of all kinds and at any moment of the day. Spending a couple of days with your best friend is a wonderful gift!"

The power of intimate friendship in marriage transcends time and space. A woman in her late seventies, widowed only a short time, shares this example. "One springtime was this past year when I found that valentine from Howard. I was wandering around feeling so bad. 'Oh, Lord,' I said, 'if I just could talk to him.' I happened to look in a drawer, and there was this beautiful valentine. Howard bought valentines, but they were usually funny. They didn't say much about how he really felt. He didn't talk about those feelings too much. But his last Valentine's Day, he gave me the most beautiful card."

Her eyes wet with memories, sparkled as she continued.

"It said: 'With love to my wife on Valentine's Day. Love is the thought of all the ways you show you care for me, your willingness to share my life, whatever it might be. Love is the thought of all the hopes and dreams we've seen come true, and every day I realize I'm more in love with you. Happy Valentine's, Darling.' And he signed it, 'Love, Howard.'

"I read that and I just perked right up. I got busy doing things around the house, and I just knew that he was still there, taking care of this crazy old woman!"

She threw back her head and laughed. "You know, we had rough times. Sometimes I wondered if I'd made a mistake or what it would have been like if I'd married someone else. We all do. But we get through those times, and isn't it great to have someone who loves you, wrinkles and all!"

After forty years of marriage, even death couldn't keep this couple's love from bringing spring into the cold winter of mourning and loneliness. They had shared too many struggles, too many victories. For forty years, they had been intimate, letting the "wrinkles" show. They had loved and had known love.

The warmth of springtime intimacy coaxes your secret parts, your "wrinkles," out into the sun of love, of God's love, shining on you through your spouse.

Everything in nature works together to bring forth new life in spring. The ice melts, and rains soften the earth. Sun warms seeds hidden deep in the soil. Their shells soften and tiny plants push up and out. Springtime intimacy in marriage is the same. Worries, hopes, and dreams that had been frozen in fear or self-doubt come rushing out like streams swollen by spring thaw. Encouraged by acceptance and love, you are free to be yourself and to discover who you are together.

PRAYER

*A*s new plants stretch upward with their leaves to embrace the energy and warmth of the sun, they reach deeper and wider with their roots, hungrily sucking up the nourishment embedded in the moist earth. This same eagerness to be open and receptive to life and love is an evident characteristic in the interaction of couples experiencing a spring season in their relationship. This enthusiasm is also characteristic of their springtime relationship with God: their prayer.

Prayer is not only "talking to God"; it is "being with God." It is the essence of a partnership with God. Being open to receive God's gift of himself, receiving the personhood of your spouse as gift, and giving of yourself are the splendid facets of couple prayer in spring.

This intimate sharing and intertwining of lives and passion, love and fidelity, make marriage an apt metaphor for God's relationship with his people. For those called to marriage, the sacrament is not only a way of living with and loving another human being. It is also a way of living with and loving God.

MARRIED LIFE AS PRAYER

Married life is prayer when it leads you to know and experience God. Married life is also a way of allowing God to touch others through your relationship. Matrimony is very much a threesome.

One couple reflects on the inscription they had engraved on their rings. "When we bought our rings, we wondered why so many couples engrave the wedding date on the inside. Surely, we would remember the date! We wanted our rings to be tangible symbols of a covenant we couldn't possibly understand, not yet anyway—and as we see now, probably never. Each journey is so incredibly unique, constantly evolving, adapting, and then beginning again. We decided to have the words 'Through him—with him—in him' engraved on our rings. It's our way of saying that ours is a marriage of three. All we were, all we are, and all we are becoming and ever hope to be are tied up inextricably with God. He is our translator, our guide in the wilderness, our hope and comfort. God is our teacher and companion throughout our lives.

"We could never have predicted that those words would be the source of strength and comfort that they have been. The inadvertent connection we made between our marriage and Jesus' act of salvation became a most powerful sign of the covenant of three."

Within your marriage covenant, your prayer life takes on an added dimension. Your individual relationship with God remains, but it is enriched and challenged by the relationship your spouse shares with God. You may find that sitting quietly in a chair listening to music is a way of entering into meditative prayer. At the same time, you recognize that a brisk walk does the same for your spouse. Together, as you journey to God, you develop and deepen your prayer as a couple.

SPRINGTIME FAITH AND HOPE

The springtimes in a couple's life of prayer are times of great faith and hope in God-with-us. They are times when the signs of God's presence—love, acceptance, and enthusiasm for a shared life—are easily recognized. Whether early in the couple's relationship or after years of marriage, this season's prayer is both the source and expression of the life of God flowing through the couple.

Within the covenant of marriage, you receive and respond to the Holy One as an individual *and* as a new creation. As a couple, you are called to be a channel of God's love and redeeming touch for each other and all those who become part of your shared life. Those times when you deepen your understanding and love for each other are also times of deepening your prayer. Letting go of personal fears and agendas and being truly present to each other require great openness and trust.

During these times, defenses are down, the focus is on your beloved, and goodness is evident. When you are freely giving of yourselves, and when you receive each other unconditionally, God's love, presence, and grace are abundant.

One couple told of such a time early in their relationship. After months of sharing and growing in love for each other, the wife felt secure enough to tell her husband about something she had experienced years ago, something that still caused her pain and guilt. She had never talked about it with anyone but felt so much love and acceptance, so much hope in her marriage, that she decided to risk telling her husband. To her great joy, she found herself forgiven and loved. She experienced not only the human love of her husband but also God's love and forgiveness through him. A burden was lifted from her heart, and her experience of God as friend and lover grew. It was springtime after a long winter.

Prayer in spring seasons brings new life and hope. "When things get bad, we hold each other, and that makes all the difference," shares one long-married man. He and his wife have faced the usual amount of joys and sorrows as they raised their children and now enjoy being grandparents. Their holding makes all the difference because it is not just the two of them physically holding each other. It is the mystery of the Incarnation at work: God uses their human love and bodies to impart his love, strength, and hope—bringing spring into their winters.

THE FRUIT OF SPRINGTIME PRAYER

The fruit of your springtime prayer is not reserved for the two of you. Within the covenant of your marriage, you serve your families and the larger community. In springtime, your prayer as a couple encompasses your immediate world and the global community. Perhaps you work together in marriage preparation or marriage enrichment; maybe you work with other parish programs or community efforts. Perhaps you're genuinely responsive to those around you. However you serve, it is God's love you share with others. In your spring seasons, you draw strength, encouragement, hope, and enthusiasm from your relationship with God.

"When my children were very young," shares Wanda, "I spent most of my day in endless cycles of cooking, cleaning, laundry, and meeting child needs. I began to wonder if I was slowly going brain-dead. I was sure I was the most uninteresting person Darian met all day. Even if I could think of something to talk about, I couldn't stay awake after the children were in bed to carry on the conversation. Darian's touch and understanding as I fell asleep with my head on his chest was surely God's reassurance that I was loved and was busy about things that mattered. It was our prayer. We sat together in God's presence, offering who we were that day, and God accepted us with compassion. At the moment, we were not aware that what we were doing was prayer, but it was."

God touches you and your world through each other. As the beauty and excitement of your relationship begins to unfold or is rekindled, you know yourself loved and accepted. Your ability to open to each other (and to others), to become available and vulnerable, and to receive, accept, and share God's love increases. Prayer in your spring seasons are times of reawakening, a coming out of darkness and into light.

We all experience times when something we have done or experienced casts a shadow over the present moment. The darkness closes us off to new opportunities for growth. That part of us becomes like a garden in winter. It becomes frozen and hard, unable to soak up the rain that falls. The water freezes or runs off to some place more receptive. But springtime thaws the earth. The garden drinks deeply of the warm rains that will nourish it and the life that lies waiting within.

God's grace is like the rain. It falls all yearlong. Sometimes we are frozen and hard. Anger, loneliness, confusion, and difficulties make us close ourselves off not only from our spouse but also from God. Spring, however, thaws us out. We become aware of the life that is within us—life within the covenant. When spring bursts forth, we once again become receptive to the love of God. Our desire to respond with love is the fruit of that spring.

No wonder the awakening of love for your spouse is also a spiritual awakening. Once again, you believe that God is with you because the signs are everywhere. "I am loved. I am held and cared for. What I think and feel are important to my beloved. Because my beloved knows and cares, I know God does too."

Your confidence in spring is grounded in faith. You may not think of God holding you, healing your hurts, and rejoicing with you, but that's exactly what is happening. You are sacrament to each other. From the beginning of your shared life, and throughout its many seasons, God's love and call to deeper love and commitment bind you together.

PRAY ALWAYS

Part of the joy of prayer is to discover it is ongoing. To pray always is not impossible. God is present with you as you go through your day. When you recognize God's presence and acknowledge it, you know a moment of spring.

One husband remembers the early courtship days with his wife. He was overwhelmed with joy as he realized that the woman he considered the most beautiful, exciting, and intelligent person he had ever met felt the same way about him! The fact that she wanted to spend as much time with him as she could echoed his own desire to be with her. "I felt as close to God then as at anytime in my life," he shares.

Such unconditional love moves us deeply. "I am loved!" What a transforming realization. When we encounter such love, we cannot help but encounter the Source of all love.

Joy and overwhelming feelings of being loved and held by both God and spouse are not reserved for the early days, however. The anticipation and enthusiasm that mark spring's return to a winter-weary world also mark the prayer of a couple emerging from a winter in their relationship. Hope returns to where doubt once eroded faith in God's presence.

"Looking back, I began to wonder if God really called us together in the first place," admits one wife as she remembers a painful time of feeling estranged from her husband. "I felt so alone." Through effort, prayer, and commitment, the relationship blossomed again, as did the couple's belief in God as an intimate partner in their marriage. They could again pray aloud together, thanking God for their renewed love. They could sit quietly or share the joy of making love and know that they lived and loved in the presence of the holy One.

Their prayer was again full of hope. They could share more than the superficial aspects of their lives; they could share their deepest, most intimate selves. They could share their relationship with God and help each other as they tried to be more open to him and his movement in their lives.

"I felt myself dreaming again of a real future together in spirit as well as physically," says the wife. "And when I dreamed those dreams, I felt so much peace. I felt like I was living life with my partner again."

Being aware of God's commitment as a partner in a sacramental marriage and feeling God's life within the relationship are great joys. Sharing the sense of resting together as a couple in God's presence is a prayer.

WHERE IS THE SEASON?

"We light a candle in the evening before going to bed," says one wife, "and share our day with the Lord. After we look back over the events of the past twenty-four hours, we pray the Our Father."

Some couples enjoy saying more formal prayers or attending special church services. For some, couple prayer is less planned. It might be a joint prayer of thanksgiving after coming through a difficult time or asking for strength to face one. However a couple shares their faith and prayer in spring seasons, it reflects an eagerness to embrace the life and promise they offer each other.

Much of a couple's prayer is woven into the fabric of their lives. It is not something done only before meals or at bedtime or on Sunday. A couple's prayer is their life together with God. It takes many forms. It can be the smile and touch that says you are important and loved even in the midst of deadening daily routines.

Just as buds on barren trees and flowers poking up through the snow are signs that life continues and is bursting forth again, joy, enthusiasm, and hope are signs of a springtime of prayer for the couple. They are signs that God's life, indeed, continues to flow through them and is ready to burst forth in new and wonderful ways.

Springtime is a season when the signs of life are easy to spot because they stand in such contrast to the winter landscape. Green plants begin to fill garden spots that had been littered with decaying leaves. Springtime prayer is likewise dramatic: joy where there had been sadness, hope where there had been none, faith where doubt was gnawing at the soul. God is indeed present. Knowing that gives the couple a surge of life and courage to begin again. As they seize the courage, their relationship deepens, and the horizons of their future spread wide before them. God beckons them into life.

Your prayer may be reading Scripture, sharing worship, sitting quietly, caring for your children, serving the larger community, or bringing God into the workplace. It will be all of these things at one time or another. It will always be your life together, a sacrament that is both a sign of God's redeeming love and a channel for that love to flow out and transform the world.

Summer

*T*he woods are heavy and green, from ground cover to crowning foliage on the trees. The creek is full of minnows and crawdads. Children, cooling off as they wade through the water, are armed with curiosity. Gardens are thick with plants bushed out over the neat paths that separated rows in the spring. Gardeners continue to tend the patch, picking fruit and pulling weeds. Thoughts turn to relaxation and vacation.

Summer recreation weaves in and out of busyness and exertion. It is a time of hard work as well as a time to vacation and "re-create." Summer is a nitty-gritty season when springtime dreams are turned into reality.

Gardeners who enjoyed hours of planning, of opening the sweet-smelling earth and planting seeds, are now busy keeping weeds, bugs, and small wildlife from devouring the plants that have taken root. This chore is different from the joy of poring over seed catalogs, but it is the necessary work that must precede a bountiful harvest.

Summer is a time of nurturing, of mixing sweat and labor with dreams and visions. Relationships are full of summer-like seasons when two people combine their minds, hearts, and energies to make their dreams a reality. Time is spent discovering and rediscovering ways to live together, to create a home that encourages intimacy as well as personal growth. Communication does not flow as easily as it did in springtime. In fact, part of summertime work in a marriage is to keep talking despite all the busyness.

Summer is a season of commitment. The gardeners who see that weeds pulled a few days before have once again reappeared have two choices: they can forget the whole project or they can continue to weed a little at a time, remaining committed to seeing the garden through to the harvest.

A couple, too, must persevere. Why do the things we once found so intriguing about our spouse bother us the most? Why do we need to work through the same difficulties over and over again? Why does a careless remark or a certain look still hurt when we know it is not meant with malice? Raising children, making a living wage, and balancing the budget are jobs that form time-consuming patterns. They are long-term tasks that, like keeping a garden, require commitment.

Gardeners may revise their vision as the summer progresses, relinquishing goals of neat, weedless rows and accepting—even coming to appreciate—a slightly wild look. Summers in a relationship are much the same; it's a time to reevaluate. Summer is a time not to quit dreaming but a time to be content with past efforts, to realize that dreams are tempered by reality. Dreams, like everything else, change and have their seasons.

Summer in a marriage also concerns children and jobs. The baby who slept contentedly in the parent's arms is the same one who keeps them awake all night, who needs help with school and the challenges of becoming an adult. Jobs demand time and energy and may not be as fulfilling or as financially rewarding as had been hoped.

Carefully woven through the work of the season is time to be refreshed. Perhaps busyness is what makes summer a time for planned vacations or changes in routine. If such times are not scheduled, activity will crowd them out. Relationship vacations need not be two weeks long or in a distant place. They can be an evening out, an afternoon in a park, or a day at the pool: any time a couple makes to get away from routine and relax together. Jesus remains faithful to your covenant through the endless, ordinary tasks that smother the enthusiasms of spring. Taking heart in this fact is the re-creating experience of summer.

COMMUNICATION

*C*ommunication in the midst of summer has a unique rhythm and tune. It often sounds like this:

"Bye, Honey." (*A quick kiss on the cheek.*) "I'll be late tonight. The meeting ran over yesterday and I'm swamped. Go ahead and have dinner without me. I'll warm something up when I get home."

"Okay. We may eat late anyway. Jessie has a soccer game and Greg's got cross-country. After that, we have to stop at the library to pick up books for his report. You might not miss dinner after all!"

"I have a meeting from three to seven on Thursday. Do you think you could get off a little early and be home with Dad? He'll need help with his medicines."

"The hospital is short on volunteers over the holiday.
Do you mind if I work an extra shift?"

These summertime conversations are short and concise.
Their purpose is to relay information and set up schedules.
How different these exchanges are from the casual exchanges
of spring and autumn. Hourlong telephone conversations,
making plans for your future, or rediscovering the qualities
which brought you together are rare in the busyness of summer.
The function of summertime communication is task oriented.

"How do you feel? What do you believe? What do you
hope?" are not the sounds of summer communication. "Are
you free Tuesday to go to open house—and by the way, the
bathroom faucet is leaking again" is the tune of summer. It is
not romantic; it is not the type of communication that lets you
into each other's heart. Rather, summer communication lets
you into each other's calendar and checkbook.

THE GOAL OF SUMMER COMMUNICATION

In the hot months that follow spring, the garden that was
once defined by neat rows of tender new leaves bursts forth
with unrestrained vigor. Gardeners have neither the time nor
the energy to be romantic or idealistic. Plants are growing and
blossoming, and fruit is ripening on the vines. Gardeners try
to keep up. Weeds need to be pulled, plants need to be
thinned and watered, and produce needs to be picked, eaten,
preserved, or given away.

Just keeping up, or at least not getting too far behind, is the
goal of couples experiencing a summer season. Wasting time
together becomes a fond memory as nudging dreams into
reality consumes more time and energy.

"We always wanted to own our home," says a husband who had become disillusioned by the reality of this particular American dream. "When we finally purchased a house, I discovered how much work it took to keep one in good shape. It was easier to call the landlord. Now, when the plumbing goes, so does our weekend and our budget...and something is always 'going.' "

Another husband reflects on the promotion he earned. "The extra money is nice, but now it's a constant struggle not to get married to my job. I take work home and work late at the office."

One mother of three young children offers this reflection:

"Part of the summertimes of a relationship to me is just the thankless, unremarkable, everyday things that fill up my days. There was a time when I looked at all these things that had to be done and wondered if they would ever get done, if they would ever be finished so I could get on to what life is all about. When I mentioned this to my husband, he simply said, 'But that is life.' "

Yes, it is life at its fever pitch of growing and becoming what it is meant to be. Life will have these intense seasons, whether it's plants in a garden, children in a family, partners in a marriage, or the marriage itself. Summers are times to nurture and support, enabling the life entrusted to you to grow, mature, and blossom. Whatever demands your time and attention during these seasons, your communication will be less personal and more informational. Discouraging as this can be, however, it is an integral part of the relationship.

Dreaming and planning alone do not get things done. They are important, but so is the labor and perseverance that make the plans come to life. This is the goal of summertime communication.

"WE ARE IN THIS TOGETHER"

A great temptation for the couple experiencing summer is to get consumed by the busyness and forget to share what they can, when they can. They don't take time to write the notes or make the calls that keep each other informed, that reassure each other, that "touches" each other across the chaos. Busy couples often forget to let each other know that they are still, in fact, lovers.

"When we were serious gardeners, we would work in the afternoons or evenings weeding and picking produce," remembers one woman married fifteen years. "We didn't talk much, but we knew we were working together."

Summers in a relationship often find a couple working at different tasks, working apart—yet together. They are building something together. They are busy, yes, but in the same garden. One may be at the office or in a classroom, while the other is running children to a game or puzzling over a leaky pipe. One retired wife may volunteer at the local hospital, while her husband offers his experience to help those in need negotiate government forms and applications for services.

All these activities help shape a relationship. They provide a physical place and/or funds to keep bodies healthy and the bill collector at bay. They keep the clothes clean, the lunches packed, and the electricity on. They allow each partner to contribute to the well-being of both the family and the community. Talking about them enriches a couple's appreciation of each other.

"Be careful," offers a woman who has weathered many summers. "Life can become noncommittal and routine. You have to regroup aims, redefine ideas of faith, rekindle your friendship, count your blessings, and recommit."

REGROUP AND UNCHOOSE

Activity can easily dictate your schedule once you get caught up in a job or community project; as the saying goes, "One thing leads to another." It's easy to accept a frantic pace as inevitable; then it's easy to forget that you did not always live with overburdened schedules; finally, it's easy to prioritize other things and neglect time with your spouse.

"Jean was involved in a group that provided assistance to those in need in our small town," shares a husband and father of four grown children. "It was a quick-response type of service. One day she'd get a call to drive someone into the city for a hospital appointment. Another day she'd do grocery shopping for someone. The next day she'd cook someone's meals. It was a great cause, but after a while, it was tough on our relationship. Her calls often came on the weekends, which were my only days off. Finally, after a couple of years, Jean decided to drop out. She got a job at the library where hours were more predictable. With that change, we had more time together. Someday she'd like to help with the service group again, but for now, we had to make a change. We needed time together to talk."

The main challenge of summer is to regroup when regrouping is needed. Summer is the time to change plans, set new goals, and unchoose commitments that are destructive to the relationship.

Looking back over the first ten years of her marriage, Ranisha shares how she and Jess changed their expectations to have more time for each other. "We'd been married a few months when Jess found a teaching job in a small town. We rented an old farm house on the wrong side of the tracks. It had a porch swing and, best of all, a huge lot perfect for a garden.

"That winter, Jess and I carefully planned our garden. Using graph paper and drawing to scale, we decided where everything would go. We were very organic and back-to-the-basics kinds of people when it came to gardening and food.

"That first summer I learned how to can. I made ketchup, pizza sauce, anything to use up those tomatoes. I don't like to think about how many zucchini passed through my hands. But it was a lovely garden. We composted what wasn't used and were ready to try again the next year.

"But the next year I had a baby—and a smaller garden. I was pleased to feed our infant son homegrown vegetables and meat pureed in the ever-present baby-food grinder. But I had lost some enthusiasm for canning. Jars of tomatoes and applesauce from the year before still filled shelves in the pantry.

"As years went by and more children arrived, our garden became smaller and smaller until it disappeared altogether. Although the food grinder got a lot of use, I bought jars of baby food along with less than whole-wheat bread and bags of cookies.

"Looking into the cupboard one evening, Jess shook his head and half-jokingly remarked 'Well, we've really sold out, haven't we?' I prefer to think of it as adapting."

Couples in summers often change plans to cope with the activities of the season. They regroup, evaluate their lives, determine what's going well and what isn't—and adjust accordingly. Some things can be changed—and some things simply have to be accepted.

WHERE IS THE SEASON?

If a couple does not take brief summer "vacations" to look at life around them, they'll soon realize that life will begin to make choices for them. One couple calls this "getting swept along with the river."

As busy as they are, summer seasons must be sprinkled with time to reflect on where you are *together,* to reacquaint yourselves with each other, to renew your commitment to work in the same garden.

Balancing re-creating with the busyness is the key. This must be why summer continues to be the season that is mentally connected with vacations and recreation. A time for "nonactivity" is carved from the midst of activity. Sometimes, however, planned vacations are anything but restorative of good communication in a relationship.

One couple remembers the start of a long-planned vacation. "As usual, we were late getting started. That alone was frustrating, but this time we were to meet with some relatives, and I didn't relish the thought of being the one to hold everyone up. By the time we had the car packed, the children had been anxiously sitting in it for an hour. Paul and I were barely speaking to each other. Within three blocks, we disagreed on which route to take. Pulling off the road, one of us got a bruised knee while angrily getting out of the car to switch drivers. It was not a very promising beginning."

Couples in the midst of a summer season need time alone. They need time to talk, to laugh, to cry, to hold hands, and to remember that they are best friends. When their initial efforts cause frustrations, as the family above experienced, they have to regroup and try again.

"We were so glad to be home with nothing special to do," shares one retired couple who had spent two weeks helping friends prepare to move. "We got up when we woke up and took our time eating breakfast and starting the day. We really enjoyed being able to do whatever we wanted—together, just the two of us."

One couple, parents of nine children, decided to set aside every Wednesday for themselves. They went to a quiet place, like a restaurant or coffeehouse, and had a bite to eat and a leisurely cup of coffee. When finances were tight, as they often were, the couple took long walks or sat in a park and talked. As the years went by, their older children became responsible for fixing dinner while Mom and Dad took off by themselves. After the children were all adults and the wife's aging godfather moved in, the couple once again claimed their Wednesday "vacations." They arranged with a friend or adult child to stay with the elderly godfather while they claimed their time together. "No matter how long you've been married, you need time to talk and be alone," they both insist.

Sometimes sharing feelings after not having had time to do so in a while is difficult. "The first night we usually spend working out the misunderstandings and frustrations that have built up," admits one husband as he talks about the occasional weekend getaways he and his wife take together. "We talk about stuff that we've let build up, stuff we've pushed aside because of everything else that had to get done."

His wife adds, "I usually need a good cry. When I get too busy, all my emotions get shoved deeper and deeper. When I finally get the chance to deal with them, they tumble out in tears. The first night things can look pretty bleak. But after we let our feelings show and talk things out, we begin to enjoy each other again and feel good about our relationship."

Couples with young children and without access to baby-sitters find other ways to make time to talk. "With only one income, we can't afford baby-sitters very often," shares Janice. "I feed the children early and get them to bed. Then Karl and I have a late dinner by ourselves. It's wonderful to be able to talk and not have to wipe up spills, answer questions, or mediate a squabble."

A couple that loves to camp keeps a tent ready and waiting in the closet. When their children are busy with other activities, they grab the tent and take off for a day.

Couples can't wait for big blocks of time together before they talk during a summer season. Instead, they learn to seize the opportunities that are squeezed in between busy schedules. They learn to make an opportunity if one doesn't come along. It needn't be fancy or long, but it needs to be for them alone.

The marks of summertime communication are perseverance and flexibility. Realizing that talking about schedules and finances are contributing to the relationship will help you appreciate the importance of those mundane—but crucial—conversations. The challenge of summer is to make the time to talk and not let the busyness take over. Re-creation of the relationship is as important as the busyness itself. Even the summertime gardener lets the weeds go for a while and enjoys the sweetness of a homegrown tomato or gets lost in a good book.

FAMILY

Summer gardens are demanding. When they flourish, they require large amounts of time. When they are beset by insects, blights, or extreme weather, they demand perseverance. Those tending the gardens have to search out and deal with the tiny culprits, carry water to parched ground, and find ways to nurture the plants through nature's challenges.

A married couple experiences similar demands whenever they live through a summer season. They are kept busy nurturing their relationship while working at their jobs, pursuing careers and interests, and being involved in community activities.

One woman talks enthusiastically about the summer season she and her husband are sharing. They have had many busy seasons raising their four children. Now, they're working as diligently as ever and enjoying every moment.

Both are artists. Without the responsibility of children at home, they are free to take more financial risks and focus their energies on developing their careers. "Our days are full. Now that the children are gone and Tom's actually retired, we put all our energy into our art. Tom occasionally teaches a class, and I help him with that. We get up early and get started. We are very much a team."

THE SEASON OF CHILDREN

Couples blessed with children are busy with changing roles and opportunities throughout their children's lives. When they accept the gift of children from God, whether biological, adopted, or foster children, the couple makes a lifelong commitment. Like their commitment to each other, they cannot know what challenges and rewards will develop. They are called to love and share life in an intimate way with someone other than their spouse. These relationships affect them in many ways. In the busyness of summer, the couple will have less time and energy for each other—yet, the relationship remains a priority among priorities. They are called to nurture other lives and relationships as well as their own.

Being entrusted with young lives is a great privilege. "Suddenly, there was a tremendous responsibility," says one father remembering the birth of his child, "to provide for a totally dependent being. We had to instill the love of God in that young life, educate him, and launch him into the world."

Gardeners watch in awe as plants emerge from seeds sown months earlier. Diligently, they provide the right environment for the new life bursting forth.

Parents, like gardeners, are nurturers in summer seasons. They provide what they can so the life God has given to their children might grow and unfold, uniquely and beautifully. Children are blessed with different interests and talents. Part of the call of parenting is to help them explore those talents and develop the discipline and skills to use them responsibly as adults.

Parents spend large amounts of time helping children with homework and providing them transportation. Their children's struggles become their own as they worry and pray with them through academic, social, and emotional ups and downs. Parents become 4-H advisers, football moms, soccer coaches, and school volunteers. Their home becomes a gathering place for friends, a safe place for children to retreat and regroup, a fitness center, an art studio, a haven for pets.

"Our house is just too small for what goes on in it," laments one mother. "But I keep remembering my parents' willingness to let us try things when we were growing up. If we were interested in chemistry, they would find some little corner of the basement that could hold a table and become a 'lab.' My sister loved to draw, so they got her chalks and paints, and Dad shared his workbench with her for a while. Now, my son's room looks like a small science museum, and the whole house is a workshop for an endless variety of projects. I'd like to keep it neater, but the opportunity for our children to experiment and try things out is more important."

Some children are born with or acquire physical disabilities or illnesses that require a great change in a family's routine. Other families have children with emotional problems or who have a learning disability. Some children, those adopted or welcomed into the family as foster children when they are older, may bring with them wounds and problems that grew out of an abusive or unstable family life. All these children are a special challenge to the parents. The demands on their relationship are great.

"The constant stress of always dealing with the problem and its consequences is exhausting," shares Rhonda, the mother of a child with a learning disability. "When I carry most of the responsibility myself, I begin to resent Leo and the traveling that keeps him from being more involved in the day-to-day routines."

Dealing with special-needs children also brings opportunities for the couple to work together, joining their efforts and prayers to best serve the needs of the child. Together, they allow God to use them to love the one given to their care and to love and strengthen each other.

Rhonda continues: "But when Leo makes a special effort to take over some of those responsibilities for a while, I appreciate him and his love for me even more. I feel relaxed. I find myself relating to our son in happier, less stressful circumstances. I feel renewed, both as a wife and a mother."

A couple need not have children to spend busy hours helping others realize their potential.

"I love children," says a retired school principal who never had children of her own, "and have worked most of my life with them in one way or another." After leaving her position as principal, she spent years substituting in schools and working at a preschool before she became director of the local school system's latchkey program. Her husband, ever supportive, lent his help when he could. For years after her retirement, she and her husband provided a place and encouragement for those still working in the schools by hosting annual gatherings for the teachers with whom she had worked.

SUMMER TESTS THE COMMITMENT

Busy schedules require flexibility. This is particularly true for a couple who is in the midst of summer seasons in their family life. Two adult personalities and schedules are difficult enough to manage. Add a few more people of varying ages, interests, and needs, and busy just gets busier. The willingness to bend, to change some plans, and to place the needs of others ahead of their own desires is important for a couple moving through these seasons time and again.

More people also means more needs. The obvious are love, education, and physical needs like food, shelter, and clothing. Providing for these affects a couple in many ways. Often the wage earner puts in long hours at a job less-than-satisfying. Both husband and wife working outside the home to meet the physical needs of the family is becoming more and more common. However a couple manages to put food on the table and keep the home running and hearts growing, the demands of summer seasons test the couple's commitment to each other and to their call to be there for others.

Sometimes the person who demands time and attention is not someone living under your roof but someone you are caring for nonetheless. "I did all her grocery shopping," says one woman as she shares the story of looking after her husband's elderly aunt. "She needed help with Medicare forms and other paperwork. I always accompanied her to doctor appointments to make sure she understood what she had to do. Between Aunt Ellen and the usual family commotion, I was always running somewhere!"

To Serve and Be Served

How does the relationship of husband and wife fit into all the work and busyness of summers with children or extended family commitments? How do couples juggle schedules packed with jobs, meetings, and volunteer work and still make time for each other? How do couples serve others while serving the needs of their covenant? A strong commitment to each other and to the presence of God with them in their covenant enables a couple's relationship to endure through even the busiest of times.

But the temptation of the season is ever present: to become increasingly involved in other activities at the expense of the relationship. Time for each other rarely makes it onto the calendar.

"He was so busy getting the new business started that we rarely saw each other." "Communication seemed so much easier in the early years of our marriage." "There are days when we barely see each other or even kiss." This is the litany of couples during the summertimes of their relationship.

In addition to the natural chaos of the season, our culture adds its own pressures. We are part of a high-motion society. Every "pastime" imaginable is made available to the family— right in the home. Some couples handle the pressure well but not without tremendous effort, effort which never loses sight of the fact that the couple's covenant is the solid groundwork on which everything else must stand. At some point, one of the partners has to stop and ask for time out. Then, focusing on themselves as lovers, the two reevaluate their choices and priorities.

One couple shared such a time when both their young children were ill. The oldest had been diagnosed with a rare disease requiring treatment similar to that for cancer. They made many trips to a special hospital in a nearby city. During this time, the mother gave birth to their second child. Elated, she was unprepared for the doctor's announcement that the baby had heart problems and would have to be sent to another hospital immediately.

"For a year and a half, we spent most of our time on the way to hospitals, in hospitals, or learning how to monitor our youngest's heart with machines at home," says the wife. "In the midst of all this, Tim was offered a coaching job that he had wanted for a long time. It would have meant moving to another city."

For Tim, the move would have been a minor adjustment. His day would remain much the same: teaching and coaching. But he knew his wife would have to leave her family and supportive friends who helped her cope with the illness and stress in their own family's life. For those reasons, Tim let the opportunity go. The love and sacrifices they were both making brought them closer together and strengthened the commitment they had made to each other.

Even the many demands of summer seasons which cannot be changed can be a source of grace and unexpected joy. Dealing with the summers of family life give you many opportunities to grow closer. You can find in yourselves and your covenant the strength and love that allow you to be for each other while you serve others. Your love grows through the challenges and hectic schedules. Tim demonstrated that in letting go the coaching opportunity.

A mother of three talks about the ordinary activities of family life and how she and her husband find themselves sitting on the couch, exhausted, but unwilling to go to bed. "We look at each other and smile. His eyes and shoulders betray a day that started far too early and would stretch into the wee hours if he tended to everything he should. I lay on the sofa, my bare feet in his lap, wiggling my toes in a way that says 'Please rub my tired feet.' Suddenly, I have a second wind. I know a new day is starting because I have my husband to myself at last.

"But there we are, two exhausted, ragged ends of a busy

day. We talk later than planned, realizing our hope of getting to bed early is fading by the minute. Yet, we're satisfied to have just these few minutes to ourselves. Finally in bed, I smile to myself and snuggle closer against his body. His love is such a comfort. He is my best friend, my lover, my husband. I just feel good knowing we're together, that we give and receive love between us and to others in our life. Those final moments of the day will catapult me into the next day."

Unexpected illness also brings the busyness and demands of summer into a couple's relationship. Steadily, God's love grows in the couple, enabling them to deal with the problems that arise.

An older couple's routine changed when a widowed relative suffered a series of small strokes. Although they were involved in community service, the couple assumed the major responsibilities involved in overseeing the person's care. Other brothers and their families and nieces and nephews did what they could to help: they visited, called, wrote brief notes of encouragement, and were supportive of both the invalid as well as the couple. The willingness of the couple to serve and the love and support given by the extended family to their elderly member were inspirations to others.

Sometimes a summer season comes when illness strikes your partner. "There is just so much to do," sighed one woman as she returned from work. Because her husband had recently been hospitalized with cancer, she wanted to economize her time in order to be available to him when he came home from the hospital. She maintained her usual work schedule, grabbed a sandwich in the evening on the way to the hospital, visited with her husband, and then returned home late in the evening to do cleaning, laundry, and planning for the next day. Her faith, her love, and her commitment to her husband and family kept her going, but she needed help. Neighboring couples set aside their own routines to lighten her load.

Whether caring for the needs of a spouse, children, relatives, or friends, summer seasons in a marriage teach the couple that the love they share is to be shared with others.

WHERE IS THE SEASON?

Children are among the most constant challenges reminding a couple that their love is not for themselves alone. Along with family and commitments to others, God calls the couple through their children and says, "This love, my love, cannot be held between two. It is for all my people. It is especially for these children I give to you, these others I bring into your family circle. Through your love for each other, they will come to know me and experience my love for them."

A friend has an old cedar plaque on her bedroom wall with the words "Love Serves" burned into it. Those words summarize the challenge to all married couples who spend much of their life serving God by serving each other and others.

Love serves. Shared between spouses, love serves us all on our journey to God. It serves our children; it serves our beloved; it serves the world. It flows out from our covenant into the workplace, the community, and the neighborhood. Because the demands of a serving love can be harsh and exhausting, summer "vacations" are crucial.

Vacations, kept reasonable and free of excessive stress, can be renewing. One mother speaks for herself, her husband, and their children when she remembers arriving at the beach for a summer vacation: "When I walked up the wooden stairs and peered over the dunes at the sea, there was an audible sigh from my spirit. 'I am not mother, wife, sister, daughter, girl scout leader, homemaker, cook...I am just part of creation.' The roar of the waves drowned out all the demands banging around in my head."

A change of pace and place allows us all to shed some of the expectations and demands of day-to-day life and get in touch with ourselves, with our God, and with each other. The setting does not have to be the ocean. One family goes to a rustic cabin in the woods for a weekend twice a year. Another family declares an occasional weekend as "time out": no laundry, no yard work, no football games, no social activities, for the entire weekend. They stock up on munchies, movies they want to watch, games, and books and have an "at home" vacation. Being together is the only agenda.

Whether a long vacation, a weekend, or a night together, recreation helps you relieve the stresses that can preoccupy you during a busy summer season. You are better able to put aside many of the concerns of day-to-day life and focus on each other. Like the summer gardeners who step back every now and then to admire the garden, you can take time to step back and look at your shared life, your family, your commitments.

INTIMACY

*T*he busyness that affects a summertime couple's communication and family life also affects their intimate sharings. One of the obvious obstacles to intimacy during these seasons is the lack of time a couple has to spend together. This makes all forms of communication difficult, especially intimacy. Intimacy requires time *and* privacy. You can talk about events, schedules, and family concerns within earshot of your children and others: Aunt Martha's visit, for example, is of interest to everyone. Sharing your deepest selves, however, requires privacy. Only within the embrace of privacy can you feel secure enough to let each other into the deepest regions of your hearts. There, in that private place, you can share joy, pain, fear, disappointment, hope. You can invite each other to look at the imperfections in your souls.

Because summer is the season of activity, a couple will seldom be totally alone when they find time to sit down and talk. Someone is in the next room; someone is waiting for help on homework problems; the phone rings. Long conversations are often held not with a spouse but with a child dealing with the dilemmas of growing up, the excitement of a date, or the frustrations of finding a job. Sometimes the needs of an aging parent infringe on a couple's time and privacy during a summer season.

This is the busyness of summer; this is the challenge of the season. Summer draws a couple's focus away from each other and toward other people and responsibilities. And this is important; turning outward is necessary and good. Love is to share. But when schedules become filled, a couple's intimacy suffers.

Hank shares the frustration many couples feel in the fast pace of their world: "We attempted a renewal of intimacy through a special retreat. No matter how hard we tried after renewing intimacy that weekend, though, we couldn't maintain it. We fell back into our world of responsibilities and patterns of activities that were set up without intimacy as an objective. Outside forces and our whole social milieu simply made intimacy difficult."

In spring, putting the relationship first is natural. Couples are eager to learn about each other. They are naturally open and enthusiastic about each other's life and insights. When a summer season comes, however, the couple finds themselves preoccupied with the demands of the present and the nitty-gritty of day-to-day life. When they do have time alone, their minds and hearts are filled with a list of things that "need" to be discussed and taken care of.

"Sometimes I need a lot of time just to empty my mind of all the agendas I carry around," shares Cathy. "I can't really listen. It may all be very routine, but until I can quit thinking about all the other stuff, I have a difficult time being present to my husband."

Besides the variety of responsibilities, "familiarity" is another force that works against summer couples to make intimacy difficult. The excitement and mystery of each other fades in the chaos of summer; the couple has heard each other's stories. Sharing simple life experiences, sharing stories of childhood, even laughing together over the shortcomings of human nature are squeezed out because the couple assumes they know each other well enough. Such sharing can't possibly be as important as staying on top of the demands of the moment. "Why share what's in my heart when I've said it all before?" "Why risk going into an issue; I know what my spouse thinks."

Couples experiencing a summer season have had time to be disillusioned and discouraged by the hard work of maintaining an intimate relationship. At any given time, one or the other may be tempted to give up; the effort to go on seems too great. Weary with effort, intimacy suffers and distance threatens.

Fortunately, a splendid dimension of the covenant of marriage is God's grace—evident at just such moments of weariness. As the third Partner, God will touch the heart of one spouse while the other struggles. "When Sheila is feeling most discouraged with how our relationship is going," shares Ben, "I believe more strongly than ever that we can and will make it work. I put in extra effort, and after a while, she recognizes my commitment and believes in us again."

Gardeners cannot expect a full harvest if they pull weeds and turn the soil only when they feel like it. Like the gardeners, the couple experiencing the busyness of a summer season cannot engage in intimacy only when they "feel like it." They can't share deeply only when it's convenient and expect their relationship to be vital and fulfilling. The hope and perseverance of one rekindles hope in the other.

THE VULNERABILITY OF SUMMER

Lovers in other seasons can listen to their spouse's dreams, fears, and questions without worrying about the ramifications for themselves. With little effort, they can remain focused on the other, intense and intimate.

When these same lovers experience a summer season, however, their intimacy is not as natural. They feel a sense of risk. "What will happen if I share? What is at risk? Will we fight? Will my spouse think I'm crazy? lazy? unfaithful? weak?"

Summertime lovers are more easily threatened by a different point of view, an interest not shared, or a change of direction. They have lived together long enough to know that even a slight change can have far-reaching effects. Because the summers of life are wearisome, lovers listen to each other with a hint of insecurity: "What does this mean for our relationship?" Dreams come at a price; fears are easily caught. While they want to listen with open hearts, with the well-being of the other first in their minds, summertime lovers feel especially vulnerable.

One couple shares the difficulty they have in talking about their different experiences of God's call in their lives. "If I were to satisfy my conscience," Phil admits, "I would sell everything I have—except what I absolutely need for survival—and give the money to the less fortunate. I have and always will struggle with the right balance between taking care of me and mine as opposed to those more in need than me or mine."

His wife, Sharon, is less comfortable with that idea and feels vulnerable whenever they discuss it. Phil's faith-sharing makes Sharon feel like their relationship and the security of all that they hold dear are at risk.

The topics need not be so dramatic. It may be something as simple—yet vital—as a fishing trip. "I had given up my preferred vacation spot so Ray and the kids could explore some place new," Alice remembers. "I missed the quiet of our usual week camping far from cities and commotion. But I was trying to respect their preferences. Shortly after we returned, though, I helped Ray get ready to spend a couple of weeks fishing with his father while I stayed home with the kids. I really wanted to be happy for him, but I was resentful. It wasn't easy to share my feelings with him. I felt petty and selfish—but I also felt taken advantage of. Finally, I wrote him a note and stuck it in his backpack, where I knew he'd find it in a few days. I told him to have a good time and relax, that I loved him, and that we'd all be waiting for him to return. I was able to let go of the resentment, but it was a struggle. Eventually, of course, we had to talk about it."

Revealing your feelings, especially the difficult feelings, and sharing what it is that generates those feelings, is to venture into the depths of vulnerability. Anything that is important to you, that is integral to who you are, can be difficult to talk about. Even in the best of times, you may find it difficult to discuss a visit to in-laws, the dilemma of how to discipline a child, a disturbing news report, the frustrations of a tight budget, or an irritating habit. But in the fullness of summer, such sharing is even more risky because the demands of life press in from all sides.

With effort, however, and with respect for the covenant you share with God, the two of you can venture into these vulnerable territories, deepening your love and enriching your intimacy. Seizing intimacy in summer gives you the opportunity to love as God loves, mirroring God's own love for humanity. Dying to self is painful and frightening, even in the little ways that may seem foolish. But God is a partner in your covenant. Knowing the limits of human nature, God showers your marriage with the grace that enables you to leap into the unknown with selflessness, faith, and love.

One husband put it this way: "God does on a grand scale what we try to do on a much smaller scale. He loves humanity in spite of our great failings and sin. One of the things marriage means is learning to continue to love and stay committed to someone who is not always very likable. When Pat gripes at me when I get home and I stay patient, I put aside my feelings for the good of our relationship. I can't do that on my own. God's love for all of us and his commitment to our marriage help me."

PHYSICAL INTIMACY

Physical intimacy in summer seasons suffers from the same demands as intimate sharing on other levels. After a day filled with stress and activity, body and mind are tired.

"When I think of intimacy in summer seasons, making love is not what comes to mind first," says Barb. She laughs and continues, "Of course, it's wonderful when it happens. But most of the time, we're just so tired. It's difficult enough to find time to talk."

Imagine the couple who crawls into bed and shares their respective days. As they hold each other in the quiet darkness, they empty their hearts of details and frustrations—and gradually realize a sweet desire for each other. Then comes a knock at the bedroom door or a cry from upstairs: "I'm sick!" "I can't sleep." "I had a bad dream." Or the phone rings...

Tired bodies, busy schedules, and interruptions are not the only obstacles to physical intimacy. When the couple has not had time to share on other levels, feelings of closeness or the

physical desire to be with each other will naturally lessen.
When a couple feels distant in other areas of their lives or
when one does not feel held on a spiritual or emotional level,
honest physical intimacy will be difficult. These feelings of
distance or reluctance may be the signal that helps a couple
realize they need to take more time to nurture their relationship and to share and hold each other on all levels. Their
responsibilities have taken more of their time and energy than
they thought.

Sometimes, as a couple clings to each other at the end of
the day, they can talk through problems and ease the distance
between them. At other times, the physical act of making love
is healing in itself. Because the hurts or wounds they carry are
so deep and unknowable, being loved and held completely
will touch spirits in ways they cannot understand.

"Sometimes when we steal a little time for ourselves and
make love, I end up crying," Linda admits a little sheepishly.
"They aren't tears of sadness, just lots of feelings I can't even
name. Vic's holding me and loving me somehow release
them. I feel renewed, like I can start fresh again."

Physical intimacy is an experience not only of the love you
share with each other; it is also a manifestation of God's
complete, unconditional love for you. At those moments, God
touches and heals what cannot be spoken. As in all dimensions of the covenant, God uses you to share his own love.
This fast pace of summer affects not only the time and ways
in which you share intimately but *what* you have to share as
well.

"We were married while I was still working and going to
school," shares Al. "June stayed home with our growing
family, and I was home very little. Even when I was home, I
was tired and usually had a paper or some assignment to
complete. On those rare occasions when I had a free day,

June would look at me and say, 'Honey, you need to relax. Just take the day to yourself. Do something you really enjoy.' It was a generous offer, but I couldn't take her up on it. I would sit and stare and think to myself, *Do whatever I'd like? What do I like? How would I enjoy spending this day?* I couldn't think of anything! I didn't even know what I enjoyed doing anymore!"

You don't have to be working and going to school to feel out of touch. Jobs, civic or church demands, children, parents, extended families, neighborhood crises, household chores, and holidays contribute to the pace that can deaden a person's spirit—and marriage.

What do you have left to bring to intimate moments if you no longer know yourself? Hurt? Yes. Emptiness? Yes. But how do you put that into words? How do you get in touch with it if the deep ache, so constant and heavy, has become a way of life?

WHERE IS THE SEASON?

When you listen to your spouse's pain as he or she admits to losing touch, you feel pain yourself. You hurt for your beloved—while feeling a stab of risk. Encouraging your spouse to take time to nourish his or her spirit, to rediscover what has been buried beneath the demands of the season, is not always easy. It means giving your spouse the gift of time. In this season when so many other needs clamor for a share of your time, individually and as a couple, carving out time seems impossible. But it is vital! Taking time for yourselves individually, creating opportunities for each other to have personal time, and taking time for yourselves as a couple cannot be delayed until it's convenient; it must be prioritized.

How difficult this is; it looks impossible and feels selfish —and our society offers little support. Putting your relationship first means making deliberate choices that give you the time you so desperately need. Intimacy will not just happen. It takes commitment and perseverance, the hallmarks of the summer season. It takes making your relationship a priority.

Without private and intimate time—separately and together—your covenant is at risk. What a wonderful gift to have an intimate lover who listens to your needs and says, "You are important to me. I want you to be whole, to sparkle with life and vitality. I want you to grow. Take time."

Reneé, remembering her husband's days in medical school, expresses the need this way: "I told Gene that we are like cups. We can only hold so much. Once we are full, we have no room to add more, even if we want to. When we try, the cup overflows. If you fill yourself up with all the details of medicine, you will have no room for anything else. You have to pour some of those concerns out to make room for other things."

Couples needing time together learn to use a variety of opportunities, wherever and however they are found. One couple used driving time for long, intimate conversations. Even their young children didn't change that routine. "After riding for a while in the car, the kids would fall asleep, and we could talk."

Stay up late or get up early to give yourselves the quiet you need together. Take a night or weekend away, send the children to a relative or friend, find someone to sit with your live-in elderly parent, turn off the television; all are ways to open opportunities for intimacy.

Intimacy in the summer seasons is the still point in the midst of swirling activity. It is a time and place to rest, to "come home" and remember who you are, individually and together. Pouring out some of those "other concerns" makes room for each other. No matter what other roles you play or demands you must meet, God continues to call you to intimacy, to himself, to each other.

Intimacy is a time of renewal, of healing, of hope. It is a time of re-creation, a time to talk and listen, to share tears or joy, to embrace and lay in each other's arms. When you open yourselves to each other, you open yourselves to God—who loves the two of you into wholeness and holiness.

PRAYER

Saint Paul says that those who are single can be wholly attentive to pleasing the Lord, while those who are married are busy with things of the world and pleasing their spouses. This could be written about couples in the midst of busy summer seasons. Family, work, and community responsibilities place many demands on a couple's time, energy, and attention. If they had to be free of those involvements in order to pray or to try to be "pleasing to the Lord," summertime couples would have a difficult time doing either.

Fortunately, with great wisdom and compassion, our God chose to become one with us. Born into our world, he is Emmanuel, God-with-us. As a result, we do not have to set ourselves apart from creation or from the involvements of marriage and family to seek the Lord or to give ourselves to serving him. Those God calls to the covenant of marriage will find much of their prayer and spiritual discipline coming from the very center of their vocation. This is as true in the commotion of summers as in the quieter seasons.

ALL FOR THE LOVE OF GOD

How can faith grow deeper when a couple is busy on so many different fronts?

Happily, a couple does not need to wait for large blocks of time to pray. Work, whether at home or in an office, in school or in a factory, can be a time of prayer. Brother Lawrence, a sixteenth-century Carmelite Brother, calls such prayer "the practice of the presence of God." It is remembering, in the midst of any activity, that God is present—fully present. Busyness was not an insurmountable obstacle to prayer for Brother Lawrence. "The most excellent method...of going to God," he says, "is that of doing our common business without any view of pleasing men and (as far as we are able) purely for the love of God."

This is not easy when a couple is shuffling children and activities and when the demands at work are tense. God *is* present, however. Remembering that God has taken on our human existence and is truly with us in the kitchen, in the classroom, in the office, on the freeway, and at worship helps us accept all weighty demands with greater love.

Living with another, fixing peanut-butter sandwiches, staying up all night with children, listening to a coworker's complaints, loving teenagers through their difficult years: these are demanding tasks. "It is how I approach the doing of these mundane things that elevates them and makes my daily work holy," comments one wife. "Life can be a prayer. Some days I'm talking all day to God, asking for help, or thanking him for some favor," says another.

One of the gifts of journeying to God in marriage is the support the couple lends to each other along the way—especially when the traveling is rough, as it often is. They can remind each other that it is God's work they are doing. They can help each other remember that God is part of their relationship, that they do not have to do everything themselves.

The prayer of a married couple in summer is often very ordinary. So ordinary in fact, that the couple often can't imagine it could be prayer at all. But Jesus says, "Whatsoever you do to the least of these, you do to me." In a covenantal relationship, the couple believes this. Though being a missionary in some faraway country or a monk in a monastery may seem like more meaningful ways to pray, God calls very few in those ways. A couple need not venture into distant lands to be evangelizers, to feed the hungry and clothe the naked. They need not rush to hospitals to visit the sick or to penitentiaries to visit the imprisoned. The living room and kitchen are replete with opportunities to instruct the ignorant, comfort the suffering, be patient, pray for others, give correction to those who need it, and forgive. Look at the spiritual and corporal works of mercy; they sound remarkably like a perfect job description for marriage and family life.

SUMMERTIME PRAYER IS WORK

Prayer doesn't always feel good. Brother Lawrence did not enjoy cooking and washing pots and pans. Forgiving when the hurt cuts deep, listening patiently, and washing dirty socks don't feel good, either. Prayer, whether for the Carmelite Brother or the husband and wife, is not always a quiet, refreshing interlude.

Summertime prayer is work. It is doing the routine things, the unpleasant jobs—all with love. Worry over or loss of a job, a severe illness, a problem at work that involves other people or a moral decision, an elderly neighbor who needs help with shopping or small chores, serving on a community board or committee: these are just a few of the many prayer opportunities that bless the life of a couple. How these opportunities are approached is what makes them prayer. Together, a couple can help each other see a chance to respond to God within each situation. They can pray together for wisdom as they make choices and decide how to respond.

"Our parish was starting a new program, and we had received calls to help on different committees," Peggy recalls. "The needs were real, and I knew we could be helpful. However, we only have so much time. Demands at work were particularly heavy for Dave, and I had become involved in our local school system. Prayerfully, we considered our church's request. I felt a bit guilty saying no but felt over-extended already. We decided not to get involved in yet more things. Through our prayer together, we realized that we were serving God's Church by being involved in commitments already made. Putting it into words between us made us more aware of all the things that service really is."

God needs workers everywhere. Summertime couples will find that their home, community, and workplace are as meaningful places of prayer as their church. Mary, pregnant with Jesus, walking through the marketplace or helping her cousin, Elizabeth, is an encouraging image for busy couples. Mary went about her usual tasks of keeping house, preparing meals, helping her older cousin, talking to the food sellers and the ladies at the village well, while carrying Jesus within. Through her ordinary tasks, the world was touched by its Savior. She must have woven her prayer throughout her day. After her child was born, as any new parent knows, she and Joseph had even more to keep them busy.

You are called to this same style of prayer, bringing Jesus into the midst of your family life, your workplace, your activities. But this is easy to miss because the chaos of summer is ever present.

"I always know when I have forgotten God's work and presence in the routines of my life," shares Betty. "I feel overwhelmed, easily discouraged. I'm quick to find fault with everyone and everything. Having lived with me for eighteen years, Jim recognizes the signs too and brings it to my attention. I don't always accept his observation graciously. But when I think about it, I know he's right."

Another wife shares a similar insight: "Usually, one of the two in a couple is stronger at certain times. This can't be viewed as a weakness but as an ebb and flow." This is as true of prayer and faith as any other aspect of married life. One often is the means of God touching the other.

SUMMERTIME PRAYER IS INTIMACY

"I woke up one night full of fear and anxiety," recalls Carol. "The kids had been sick for a week, and I was beginning to feel sick myself. All the concerns and worries of the past week grew larger in my mind. My mind was spinning from one dilemma to another, real or imaginary.

"I reached for the old rosary beads hanging on the bedpost. Their familiar feel and the repetition of the prayers often helped calm my spirit—but not that night. I cried. The sobs shook my whole body. I didn't know what else to do. Life seemed impossible. I felt small, helpless, and alone.

"Then Ed woke up; he felt my body shaking. He hugged me and then went and got the thermometer. When he put it in my mouth, I felt like one of the kids. I couldn't breathe through my nose! We laughed—and then we talked. Ed always knows the right things to say at times like that. Being so close, hearing his calm voice, feeling his arms around me, all broke the cycle of anxiety I hadn't been able to break myself. He didn't have all the answers, but I could feel the tightness drain out of me while he held me. We made love, and afterward, as we rested together, I knew things would work out. Later, when I thought about that night, I knew God had been with us. He had renewed our faith as we loved each other. The next day I felt as if a weight had been lifted from my shoulders."

That is the gift of intimacy in marriage. Lovemaking is one of the most intense experiences of God's love a couple can share: total giving and total receiving. Someone once said to me that making love was being "sacramentally disposed," and that's true. When lovers love in the midst of busyness, they open themselves to God's outpouring of peace. Resting with each other afterward, they rest in the healing arms of God. And that is prayer.

Another wife shares this reflection: "Marriage mirrors God's love for us, although I don't exactly think about it like that all the time. But when I'm feeling spiritually dry, I close my eyes and feel my husband's presence enveloping me. I remind myself that God's presence, acceptance, encouragement, admonishment, and love are channeled to me through this man he has gifted me with. God knows that putting a face, arms, and a voice on his love will bring us closer to him."

The more in touch with God you are, the easier it is to recognize God in your spouse. In summer that can be especially difficult. Making that time, however, is as important to your relationship with God as taking time for each other is important for your relationship. Time for prayer together nourishes the relationship of the three involved in the marriage covenant: husband, wife, and God. For many, that may be going to church on Sunday. It may be a Bible-sharing or prayer group. It may be prayers over the children or with each other at night. It may be prayer with each other in times of great joy or sorrow.

INDIVIDUAL SUMMERTIME PRAYER

Prayer time for the individual is important, too. Just as sharing intimately with your spouse is enriched if you take time to remember who you are as individuals, your prayer life with your partner grows stronger as your individual prayer life deepens. As with prayer together, individual prayer takes many forms, depending on one's personality, schedule, health, and personal relationship with God.

Large blocks of time for such prayer are often difficult to find in the summer seasons—naturally. Taking "spiritual vacations" can help renew that aspect of your lives, together and individually. Retreats, parish missions, an evening set aside to share Scripture or to share with each other how you're feeling in your relationship with God, are all ways to add depth and life to your prayer.

While special times for prayer are important, a couple's prayer in busy summer seasons is woven through the activities of their lives. The time they take to reflect, to pray alone or together, is often a time to look back on and recognize where God has been present in the ordinary events of daily routines.

WHERE IS THE SEASON?

You will find opportunities for prayer and spiritual
discipline in the midst of the demands of living intimately
together. Learning to recognize these opportunities and God's
immediate presence helps you realize that prayer can be very
much a part of daily life. One woman, married thirty-four
years, says, "Our faith just seems to get deeper, even though
we're so busy."

Parenting is one area of a couple's life together that calls
them to prayer. "The responsibility and influence of parents
in raising children, to this day, seems overwhelming," says
Paul, a father of three. Every stage of parenting seems overwhelming. It is also an opportunity for a couple to entrust
their children to the care of the Creator of all life.

"I'd had another heated argument with our oldest,"
remembers Rita. "I was sure I was doing everything wrong
when it came to her. I had lots of questions but no answers as
I tried to figure out what to do to get her on the right path. I
sat and worried. Then John offered his thoughts: 'We're
doing our best, you know.' I didn't find that helpful; our best
wasn't proving good enough it seemed.

"That's how the conversation went for a while. Finally,
John said, 'We can't do it all, Rita. You have to trust God. He
loves us. He loves our daughter. Every day we'll try our
best—and pray.'

"And we did pray. Although there were no magical
changes, I could rest, at least for a while, knowing that we
weren't alone, that we could trust our family to God's care. I
could let go of my desire to be in control of the situation. Our
prayer helped me accept my limitations and have faith that
God would fill in where we were lacking."

When you feed your family, bring home a paycheck, help

with homework, share your faith with your children through prayer and family rituals, keep the beds and towels clean as the flu moves through, hurt with and listen to your spouse, wait for your adolescents until they're ready to talk, take food to grieving families or the Eucharist to the homebound; when you do these things for your family, for your own small communities, you are doing them for the Lord. He is in you and in your spouse. Being with him, serving him in these tasks done with love, is surely prayer.

Do not look wistfully for days when you'll not be so busy with family or job. Rather, realize that right in the midst of the busyness of summer is where you will find God, smiling and waiting. When you are tempted to think that your life as a spouse and parent is too much concerned with things of the world to be concerned with God, remember Brother Lawrence's prayer: "My God, since you are with me, and since it is your will that I should apply my mind to the outward things, I pray that you will give me the grace to remain with you and keep company with you. But so that my work may be better, Lord, work with me; receive my work and possess all my affections. Amen."

You have many responsibilities—but you also have a special gift of experiencing God-with-us: you have each other!

Autumn

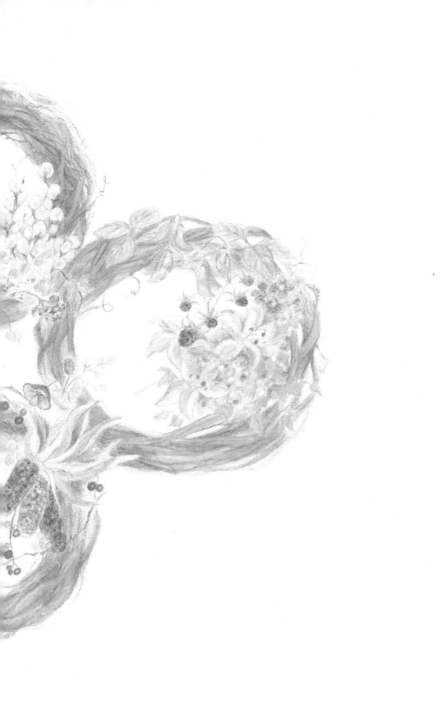

*T*he coolness of autumn is invigorating. Even when the days are warm, they lack the stifling humidity of midwestern summers. After a frost or two, evenings can be enjoyed without many insects. Burnished leaves hang overhead and crackle underfoot. The woods welcome the hiker without summer's dense undergrowth.

Gardens may still produce fruit but not at the intense pace of summer. Plants die a quiet, natural death, a graceful giving up to the earth what will become the soil for next year's crop.

Autumn is a time to relax and enjoy the fruits of summer's labor before the chill of winter arrives. Harvests are almost complete. In a relationship, autumn is a restful time. Free— perhaps for only a fleeting moment—of summer's activity, a couple can relax with each other and savor some uncomplicated moments of joy. When difficulties arise in autumn, the couple is not overwhelmed with the challenge. Instead, they respond with confidence and faith, working in harmony. For a brief moment, for several days, perhaps even several weeks, the couple knows a smooth synchroneity.

Summer's business and preoccupation with tasks to be done are offset by autumn's harvest: a time to enjoy the fruits of hard labor. Our local county fair is held in the fall. An entire building is filled with tables and displays of fruits and vegetables, jams and jellies, bread and cakes. Farmers and young farmers-to-be show their livestock. Food stands sell apple cider, roasted corn ears, and a wide variety of foods. Those who have been busy all summer raising the crops, caring for the animals, preparing recipes, and finishing projects, come to wander through the fairgrounds. Proud of their own work, they can also appreciate the work of neighbors and friends. It is a celebration of the bounty of summer's labor.

The autumns in a relationship are times for the couple to enjoy the fruits of all the tears, fears, prayers, and efforts of other seasons. Summer demands have lessened. Winter chill is yet to come. The gifts of God in the relationship are easy to see and experience: acceptance, love, balance, the sense of being together on the journey—together and with God.

Autumn is an interlude, a gift that refreshes the spirit.

COMMUNICATION

*A*utumn is a time to catch your breath between the busyness of summer, the struggles of winter, and the enthusiasms of spring. The first crisp days and cold nights set our spirits soaring and move our hearts to song. Autumn's vivacity differs from the eagerness of spring. It is not so much a looking forward to what is coming as a time to enjoy the moment.

The same is true for a couple experiencing an autumn season in their relationship. It is a time of balance when they are able to appreciate each other in the moment. They are not preoccupied with problems, pressures, and schedules.

Nature's pace slows in the fall. Weeds are no longer outgrowing the vegetables. Tomatoes and zucchini have, thankfully, quit producing. For the gardener, that means increasingly less time is spent tending the plants, weeding, and harvesting. Eventually, the gardener will be content to watch while natural forces take over.

The more relaxed pace of autumn affects a couple's

communication. Time to talk is not squeezed between a rush of other activities. Talk flows at a steady pace, much like a stream that passes over rocky falls, riffles, and then broadens for a while, smooth from bank to bank. Fish and wildlife find shelter and home in its cool, deep expanse.

A couple experiencing this season in their relationship is comfortable with silence. One woman, married thirty-four years, shares this thought: "Sometimes we're just quiet. Neither one of us feels we have to be talking all of the time, thank God! We both are good listeners with each other...."

Another writes: "I say this not only because autumn is my favorite time of year but also because our relationship has grown to the point that we are much more appreciative, mellow, and comfortable with each other. We know each other's thoughts and feelings almost as well as we know our own, but we still have the ability to pleasantly surprise each other and therefore bring a freshness to our marriage, much like the crisp air of autumn."

When a husband and wife have worked through various seasons together, they can often communicate without a word. Catching each other's eye as they move through a noisy party or a crowded meeting can say *I love you; I know what you're thinking; isn't this crazy; I can't wait till it's over!* Sometimes a slow, gentle touch on her husband's shoulder as she walks by or a hand squeeze as they attack a mess in the kitchen or a room to be painted, can say, *I'll be glad when we have some time to ourselves* or *I'm thinking of you. I know you're tired.*

THE AUTUMN SIGNALS

A couple enjoying an autumn season is better able to recognize signals and read between the lines.

"I used to get worried when Bob talked about dropping everything and going back to school," says Milly, married ten years. "I would listen and think about all the changes that would mean for the rest of us. My first reaction was to voice all those concerns, fearing he'd already made the decision. Now, I know that when Bob talks like that, he's mainly letting off steam or reacting to a particularly difficult time at work. I don't feel threatened, and I realize that if he were seriously considering a move like that, we'd talk it over and make decisions together."

Barry shares this story: "When we're trying to talk and getting nowhere, I take a closer look at Val. She's often tired and grouchy, just worn out from her busy day. I used to take her mood personally, thinking she just didn't want to talk to me or didn't like anything I said. Now, I try to give her a smile and suggest she go to bed and get some sleep!"

Couples communicating in this season are able to discern when an issue is important and needs attention—and when the issue isn't especially crucial. A curt reply or unwillingness to talk may be the result of fatigue or frustration. It may be a sign of deeper problems that need loving attention. Clear thinking and the ability to recognize a genuine need in the other are gifts of the season. Being able to enjoy brief autumn moments as well as longer stretches of time when communication flows comfortably are results of innumerable hours spent striving to express thoughts and feelings when circumstances are not favorable. The couple falls back on the fruits of tending to their relationship through the other seasons as best as they could.

Being honest with each other and admitting difficulties as well as successes help keep communication going. In the other seasons, when communication isn't perfect, the couple's willingness to keep trying brings the harvest of sweet communication in autumn. "It's refreshing to see how calmly we can handle a situation that might have caused problems before," shares one couple. "Having kept lines of communication open, every now and then we experience a plateau, an unpressed, pleasant time when communication is easy and natural." That is communication in autumn.

A young wife reflects on the emotions she dealt with facing surgery and possible cancer: "Had this happened when we were at a different place in our relationship, I might have fallen apart. But this time our relationship was strong and intact. Communication was very good, and intimacy was a source of strength and comfort." That is communication in autumn.

A TIME OF RENEWAL

Autumn is a time to renew resources. A gardener uses some of the time freed from summer tasks to preserve the abundance of harvest, putting it away for use in the winter months ahead. During this season, a couple enjoys life together, gliding over the ups and downs and deepening their appreciation for each other. Later, they will draw on these experiences and memories to help them through less peaceful days. When times get hectic, lonely, or cold, the couple will draw on the integrity of their relationship and trust their history together. Autumn memories and experiences will be a source of strength and hope.

A couple can take advantage of autumn calm to search their hearts and find parts of themselves that have been neglected in other seasons. Disappointments, hurt feelings, and fears that had been put on hold can be shared and healed, strengthening the partners and their relationship for the busier times.

"Finally! Soccer season was over and the dance recitals were finished for the year," says Brenda with a smile. "We quit having dinner at Wendy's in between stops. Stan and I had time to share our feelings about plans for placing his uncle in a nursing home. We both had gone through much personal soul-searching and had mixed feelings. We just hadn't been able to talk about them with each other. It was a relief when we could. It seemed like a shadow had lifted, and we could move forward knowing we had each other's support."

SOME DYING...

Autumn is a time of dying and letting go. In a garden, the plants give up fruit as their last act, then go back to the earth to nourish next year's growth. A couple experiencing this season become comfortable with the dying and giving up they do as individuals. They know that the dying will nourish the relationship. One husband who enjoys involvement in community theater lets many auditions pass, knowing the commitment of time and energies required is often too great for his already busy wife and family to absorb. The sacrifice is not only for the spouse but for the marriage as well—a priority for both.

Letting go of unreasonable expectations is also a mark of autumn. Couples accept where they are and what they have fashioned together at the moment. It may not be their ideal, but it is the product of their best efforts.

One husband shares his struggle to accept a less than ideal schedule, knowing that the situation would eventually change: "We always ate dinner together and valued the time as an opportunity to talk. But that changed when I had to take a different shift at work. We didn't like eating alone, but it couldn't be helped. Instead of complaining about it and resenting the intrusion, we found other times to be together and reminded ourselves that it wouldn't last forever."

...AND SOME RISING

Trusting that Jesus is truly a partner with them in their marriage helps a couple become more accepting of their lives together. They are able to let go of some goals and hopes because they believe in spring, in new life to come. Such faith makes the dying and letting go graceful.

The couple experiencing autumn is at peace with the cyclic nature of their relationship. They need not strive after or grasp goals that must be relinquished. They know other goals lie ahead; other seasons will come. There will be more summers of growth, more spring dreams, more winters, more autumns.

A couple hasn't been able to buy the larger house they had hoped for, but its importance fades when they focus on other riches they have as a family. A career has been interrupted to raise a family, but the initial struggle is over and both partners enjoy their new roles. Early marriage adjustments are difficult, but the couple ventures into autumn to give rise to their own mutual traditions and expectations. Together, they settle into a "coupleness," developing their own routines.

All are examples of an autumn-like willingness to enter into the moment with a quiet confidence in the ability of the relationship to meet the future as it unfolds. The absence of anxiety and preoccupation with planning and control gives the couple time to enjoy the reflective quality of autumn. In autumn, the gardener looks over the plot of earth, now overgrown, and remembers the spring planting and the hard work of summer. The gardener laughs, remembering the attacks of ground hogs and rabbits—attacks that weren't so funny at the time. The gardener remembers the harvest.

A couple looks back together over other seasons they've shared: a recent spring when they were full of enthusiasm, a busy summer. They laugh over some of the difficult times they've been through—and survived! Sharing the memories reassures the couple that after the dying, there is, indeed, the rising, a sweet gift of the season.

WHERE IS THE SEASON?

I walked into the home of an older couple who had been married fifty-four years. I carried a small plate of homemade hot cross buns. My husband, children, and I were going on a spring-break trip, and I wouldn't see the couple for several weeks. As usual, the gift was accepted with much enthusiasm.

"We're going to Washington, D.C.," I said.

"Oh! How wonderful. I'd love to be going on a trip," May said.

"Now, May," admonished her husband, "we've had lots of trips. It's time for someone else to have a turn."

And then they began to remember together. They told me about the trip when someone forgot their shoes and they had to turn around and come back. They remembered their own trips to Washington and the many times they met at a rooming house in a small town when the husband's job caused him to travel a great deal. They remembered family vacations and drives to visit friends. Together, they remembered and derived joy again from roads traveled a quarter of a century ago.

Although they didn't know it, their remembering was a gift to me. Remembering is an autumn gift to all couples: the opportunity to reflect, to remember, to enjoy again—together.

Often the days and weeks following a holiday are an autumn experience. The hustle is gone, schedules return to the routine, and there is time to reflect. There is time to plan for the future and enjoy the present again.

"I came home from work early one day," shares Charles. "It was only a few hours before the school bus would bring the children home, but it was enough time for Donna and me to enjoy a quiet lunch and some good conversation. We caught up on some exciting work I had been doing but hadn't had time to share. Short as the time was, we were glad to know we could sit together and enjoy each other's company—no big problems pressing to be solved, just easy conversation."

One couple built a little autumn into every day while their children were young. They declared the hour before dinner as their time. The children knew to busy themselves somewhere besides the living room. That was their parent's domain for sixty minutes.

"We delivered my report to the office and then spent the afternoon at the art gallery," said one wife as she thought of an autumn moment. "Nothing special, just some quiet time together to enjoy a mutual interest."

During autumn, a gardener has time to review last year's efforts and learn from the process for next year's sowing. A couple looks back at their experiences in other seasons and together extract the wisdom they can. The next time they are in the midst of summer, winter, or spring, they will be a little wiser.

The last thing gardeners do in the fall is prepare the soil for the winter. They pile on autumn's leaves for mulch to be plowed under in the spring. They cover plants or take indoors the delicate ones that need protection from harsh temperatures. Finally, they gather seeds that will be sown with the first thaw of spring.

In the same way, the couple uses autumn to prepare for future seasons. They become familiar again with what they know and are capable of doing: communicating. Using their communication skills to foster companionship, trust, and intimacy, they reaffirm themselves and each other. They know they have journeyed through many seasons together to be enjoying this season, and they remind themselves that they can weather many more.

FAMILY

We have all known the sweet, luxurious feeling of having finished a large task or survived a particularly difficult period in our lives. Sinking into a favorite chair or taking a leisurely walk, we relish the moment. For a while, we have the gift of time, unencumbered, to use as we like. This is autumn.

"It's so good to be home!" sighs the executive who has finished two weeks of travel. The sentiment is echoed by the parent who has no school sports event or activity on the calendar, the convalescing patient who has returned from the hospital, the parents of the bride who have said good-bye to the last guest and are peeling off their formal attire.

Autumn is that time: a time to let go. This may not necessarily be in the literal sense, although it often is. When a busy family has a break between scheduled activities, letting go is a refreshing experience.

Autumn is a time when we are mentally and spiritually

present to each other as life partners, friends, and lovers. Focusing our attention on those close by, we hear and we listen, embracing them with our hearts.

THE NATURAL RHYTHM OF AUTUMN

For the family, autumn finds day following day without major upheaval. Family life finds a natural rhythm and falls into place without excessive commotion.

This interlude means many things. You have the luxury again of wasting a little time together. Your children and friends see you taking pleasure in each other's company, enjoying life in a relaxed way that is often crowded by busyness and stress in other seasons. Just as tension and unrest between the two of you filter into your family inter-action and routine, so does the calm and peace you share in the autumn season.

"One morning I noticed a new picture hung on our refrig-erator gallery," says Anne. "Drawn by our seven-year-old daughter, it had two birds sitting on a branch. The words 'Love Birds' were scrawled in large shaky letters across the bottom. When I asked her about it, she said, 'I know you and Daddy love each other.' Paul and I had recently made a retreat together and were experiencing a renewed sense of closeness and joy in our relationship, but I had no idea it was so obvious to our children!"

THE HARVEST

Besides having the time and inclination to enjoy your own relationship, autumn gives you the time to step back, to recognize the fruits of your labor, to reap the harvest. Like the gardeners who harvest and savor the fresh fruits and vegetables they have tended all year, you delight in the growth and accomplishments of your children. Whether you delight in the antics of a toddler or marvel at the maturity and independence of an adult child returning from the first year of college, you experience a sense of joy and fulfillment.

"We felt so happy after the last conference with our son's teacher," shares one husband. "He had been having so much trouble at school. Besides having a learning disability, he had difficulty getting along with the other kids. All the tears, effort, and prayers of the past months seemed to have born fruit at last! After sharing the good news with our son and getting him to bed, we just sat together in the living room enjoying the respite from so much worry and hard work."

"Our children are our treasures," wrote one woman whose children are all now adults. "The kids are wonderful, and we knew it while they were all underfoot. They are still very attached and in touch."

Visiting grown children and their families is a great source of joy for many couples. Some look forward to vacations spent with such extended families. Others are able to enjoy their adult children more frequently. "How wonderful it is to have our grown son drop by for lunch and talk about the things he and his family are doing," says Bernice. "We enjoy him and are pleased that he stops in so often. Frank and I laugh when we think about how much trouble he was through high school. Those were not easy years, but all the effort was more than worth it!"

Occasional family weekends away together are autumn-like times for others. "We rent a little cabin located in a wooded hollow south of town," says one husband. "We stock up on food— snack food mostly—games, books, and plenty of logs for the fireplace. Then we just hole up for the weekend. No phone, no TV, no distractions. Cares and concerns about school, job, lack of money, even the four food groups: none of that is allowed to come along. We retreat and just enjoy being a family. One time an ice storm hit and we were stranded. It was great."

Having time to do nothing special is a gift of autumn. "Some things that have resulted in a special blessing with our children have been nature walks, bike rides, reading and discussing books—and just talking," volunteers a busy father. "Overall, the best thing we do as a family is just talk and listen to one another."

A couple often experiences a sense of autumn peace and fulfillment after they accomplish something together. It might be building a house or an addition and moving in, finishing school and getting a new job, working through a strained time in their relationship, or something as simple as keeping a weekend wonderfully "unbusy."

Some couples experience an autumn season when they reach out to others. Not needing to devote so much energy to keep their own relationship going, they offer to participate in marriage-preparation programs in their parish or diocese. Some host a special evening for couples. Others find that their interlude of calm and enjoyment is attractive to others and can offer encouragement and hope to those who ask. Aware of the blessing of the season for their marriage, the couple might keep all those called to matrimony in their prayer.

SOME DYING...

In the calm and contentment of autumn, dying and letting go can happen naturally. For some couples, autumn brings the image of children leaving home. That can be true, but autumn is also a time of letting go of one way of living while a new one unfolds. Autumn is a time of metamorphosis. Children arriving as well as leaving mark a time of transition. Changing jobs, moving, illness, and other major changes require a couple to do some dying to familiar routines as their lives take new directions and face new challenges.

A couple does not wait until their children are old enough to leave home to learn to "let go" of them. As children grow older, they need less—or different—time and attention. As a result, the couple can direct more energy into other pursuits.

One wife, married over thirty years, shares these thoughts on married life after their children had grown: "Through the years, we maintained a best-friend relationship. Now as our children leave the nest, it is just the two of us again. We're enjoying each other much more deeply than ever before.

"All that said, though, I admit that a certain unforeseen aspect has entered into our blissful season and has created not too few adjustments in our serenity. Our youngest son is now living at home again until he can be totally on his own. The fact that another adult, albeit an offspring, has invaded our 'space' has shown us a need to draw from the well of tolerance and patience. It has not made for an easy coexistence at times, but we fall back on our faith, love, communication skills, and sense of humor. That's how we've always gotten through things."

Another couple, married thirty-eight years, experienced the mystery of dying to one way of life in order to pass into a new one when they sold their family home: "We are selling our big family home, so dear to us, so many memories. But we're excited about our new home, fixing it up to suit us so it reflects our personalities and our lifestyle."

...AND SOME RISING

As you let go of some familiar routines, some personal desires, and some expectations, the struggle passes—at least for a while. You let life unfold and trust in God's providence, in the love you share as a couple, and in your ability to cope. Autumn is a season when you accept your inability to be in control. Unable to see what is best or to determine the ultimate outcome of the challenges you face, your faith in each other and in God-with-us enables you to be comfortable with what comes.

Autumn is also a time of renewing resources. Special vacations, enjoyable mealtimes, and family gatherings are opportunities to build memories that will carry you through more difficult seasons. When family life is strained, you can draw encouragement from your memories of times when relationships and schedules flowed with less turbulence. Those times remind you that understanding and harmony have existed before and can again; they give you hope to keep trying.

"I remember Mom's seventy-fourth birthday," shares one woman. "Most of my brothers and sisters and their families were there. Some of us sat in the living room trying to watch the Olympics through the web of giant Tinkertoys the cousins were playing with. It was the usual controlled bedlam. Some were talking around the kitchen table, others were playing pool in the basement. Everyone had a good time, from the youngest to the birthday honoree. Something about the security of the family, of the variety of people and interests meshing together for the evening, gives me hope when we run into difficulty in our family. I know that we have great strength together and can count on support when times get rough."

Autumn gives you the time to reflect, to appreciate the gifts of special moments that you may otherwise miss in another season. A gardener uses autumn to look back over the efforts of spring and summer, to discern what contributed to the success of the harvest, to learn from mistakes. A couple experiencing this season, like the gardener, has the opportunity to remember together and to recognize the gifts they have been given.

WHERE IS THE SEASON?

"An autumn moment for us is looking in on the children before we go to bed," shares one woman with a smile. "In that quiet moment, we remember the little things they've done, the 'battles' they've fought that day. We see them for the gift they are and pray for wisdom as we help them grow. Right then, spilt milk and angry words fade. They are people God has given us to love."

Sitting outside in the evening—any time of year and in any kind of weather—is an autumn moment for another couple. Watching homemade videos and looking through picture albums, baby books, and scrapbooks are all times to reflect and appreciate times together. Birthdays and anniversaries, sending someone off to college, or planning a wedding are times for couples and their children to share stories. "Remember when...." "What did I look like when I was a baby?" "How did you and Dad meet?" are all good beginnings for autumn moments in the family.

"My widowed aunt spent many of her last years researching and writing a family history," shares one fortunate young woman. "She included anecdotes as well as dates and family trees, so the people that fill its pages are 'alive' to those of us who never met them. What a treasure she has given to us all. She took time to look back at our family history, and now we are able to share it with a new generation. The stories give us a strong sense of rootedness and belonging."

Autumn gives you time and energy to reflect on family stories, to enjoy the moment together, to take pleasure in the relationships you have worked diligently to build.

INTIMACY

*I*ntimacy in autumn is not the struggle it can be in winter and summer seasons. Nor is it the intense, all-pervasive force it can be in spring seasons. Autumn intimacy is comfortable. It's like those old shoes that you don't make a big fuss about and would be lost without. Those shoes get you through long days when you're on the go; they hold your feet in blissful comfort after a day of wearing stiff, pinching shoes.

After periods of estrangement and difficulty, or after particularly hectic seasons when time together was almost impossible to find, autumn intimacy is welcome. It flows easily through the days, making life sweet and peaceful. The couple's closeness helps them meet challenges and crises with an even spirit. Sharing is natural for a couple in autumn.

Taking pleasure in this type of intimate sharing is the result of much effort, trust, and perseverance. A gardener enjoys an abundant harvest after seasons of planning and hard the season only after faithful effort through more difficult times.

AUTUMN'S UNDERLYING CONFIDENCE

Seventy-eight-year-old Page remembers the joy of growing old with Howard, her husband. Like all couples, Page and Howard had stormy periods, times when they wondered if marrying each other had been the right thing to do. "I could have married a rich young man," Page says with a smile, "but I chose Howard." Memories of the uncomplicated intimacy of their later years made her eyes shine. "As I look back on my marriage, I think the later years, when Howard was retired and we had so much time together, might have been our best. As you grow older, you have to have somebody to laugh at the wrinkles, the stiffness in your joints, your fatness. But, oh, how you love the feeling of those warm arms and feet as you slide into bed at night!"

Sharing your deepest self is easiest when you are comfortable with who you are. Whether seventy-eight and married forty years or twenty-five and married two, you are able to share intimately in a relaxed way when you're comfortable with yourselves and your relationship. Page knew Howard would put his arms around her when she slid into bed. She would be welcomed and loved just as she was.

During autumn, each partner feels an underlying confidence in themselves, their marriage, and God's presence in the relationship. They are confident of being accepted for who they are. They know they are seen as a person with something meaningful to give. Autumn intimacy is a freeing experience, one that encourages deep sharing.

Once my daughter was invited to a birthday party for a

classmate she did not know well. We had a difficult time choosing a present for two reasons. First, of course, she wanted the gift to be something her classmate liked. Not knowing the child, however, made it difficult for her to make that choice. Second, my daughter wanted the gift to be something the other children at the party would admire, something that would make her feel more a part of the group. She wanted to give something valued by others. She wanted very much for both her gift and herself to be enthusiastically accepted.

A few weeks earlier she had been invited to a party for her best friend. She went shopping with enthusiasm, knowing what she wanted to get. "Angie is creative. I think I'll get her some Sculpey modeling clay. She can make all kinds of things. She'll love it!"

No hesitation there. Neither was she concerned about what the other guests would think of her gift. She knew Angie would like it. She was confident of their friendship and didn't need the approval of the others to bolster her sense of belonging.

"Autumn is being content together, without words," explains one woman. "It's knowing that you made the right choice—and at such a young age. If nothing else does, that convinces me that there are three of us in this together!"

It is easier to give a gift when you feel good about it; the giving is made even easier when you give it to someone you know cares for you and has received your gifts lovingly before. The same is true in your marriage when you are giving the most precious gift of all: yourselves. When you're confident and know you have something valued to share, you're more willing to give it. After years of revealing yourselves to each other, of sharing your hopes, dreams, fears, and bodies, you feel safe. You're even eager to further entrust yourselves to each other.

Giving a present to her best friend was a simpler, freer act for my daughter than giving one to an acquaintance. The same is true for spouses. When their friendship is strong and their faith in the relationship is firm, intimacy is gentle and unconstrained.

"Now that our children are gone and married and all live out of state," says a woman married over thirty years, "we share on a daily basis. We are each other's best friend."

THE INTIMACY OF LOVERS

Physical intimacy flows naturally from the closeness of married "best friends" who know themselves as lovers in the season of autumn. Like intimacy on other levels, the physical intimacy the couple shares is comfortable and free. They know how to please each other. As they grow and change, they talk without embarrassment about what feels right. Not worried about "performance," the partners experience lovemaking as a joyful celebration of the closeness they experience in all dimensions of their shared life.

The couple's physical intimacy is also a celebration of the closeness of God drawing the couple not only to each other but to God himself. The willing acceptance of each other, the joy in sharing their bodies, the tenderness and oneness they feel, celebrate the all-encompassing love of God.

Couples experiencing an autumn season physically convey their feelings for each other in many ways other than sexual intercourse. Their deep-seated sense of intimacy is communicated with a touch of hands or a tender caress. Having shared so completely before, their oneness finds expression in simple gestures that for them become imbued with a deeper, spiritual meaning.

In her book *Two-Part Invention: The Story of a Marriage,* Madeleine L'Engle describes such expression of intimacy shared with her husband during his battle with cancer.

"I go to my lonely bed, thinking of Hugh alone in his hospital room, grateful for the nurses who are so good to him. During the night, I reach out with my foot through force of habit to touch his sleeping body. And he is not there. Nevertheless, we have been making love during this time in a profound way. He is making love with me in the pressure of his fingers. I am making love when I do simple little bodily services for him. How many times he has taken care of me! And that is intercourse as much as the more usual ways of expressing sexuality."

SOME DYING...

Autumn is a season of dying and letting go. Expressions of intimacy change as couples change, as their relationship changes, and as life circumstances change. A couple in the season of autumn might experience intimacy in new activities they share together, letting go of those that are familiar and comfortable.

...AND SOME RISING

Relinquishing some freedom of intimate expression is something couples encounter when children arrive. Although the partners give up some spontaneity, they find a new awareness of their love for each other through their children. The woman feels deeply loved as she listens to her husband reading to the children or watches him fix a kite or work on a car with a teenager. The man feels the love of his wife as he watches her comforting their child, helping a son work through an algebra problem, or tying a young one's shoe. Couples in this season of their relationship recognize love in the actions of their spouse, whether done for them or for others.

"I sit in the theater and watch my husband on stage," says one wife. "I know he's good. I know he's sharing his talent with the community, inviting us all to ponder the truths, mysteries, and complexities of life. It's a gift, and as I watch him, I become more aware of who he is. I appreciate him and feel my love grow. Even though it's him on the stage, I know the play involves us both, and I feel the bond between us deepen."

A husband has similar feelings as he sees the hours his wife spends preparing a special classroom project for her students. One wife says her feelings of closeness grow when she listens to her husband talk about his day at the hospital or sees his quick response to an emergency call.

WHERE IS THE SEASON?

Autumn is a time when confidence in your relationship allows you to watch and enjoy the personal growth and achievements of each other. As you see more and more of the treasure God has placed within your relationship, you rejoice deeply in your connectedness.

"Even little moments count when we are feeling close," comments one wife. "We feel free to talk about anything without wondering how we'll be received. Excitement about a bird we saw in the backyard, wondering about a job offer— whatever we share brings us closer together because we know we're giving a part of ourselves. A walk, holding hands, a kiss: they all deepen our caring for each other."

"Autumn is the awe we feel in each other's arms," says a wife of eighteen years, "the times when our relationship seems to be pure gift. The more times like that we have, the less unsettling are the winters or summer seasons." This experience of the relationship as a gift to be treasured, as a closeness to be enjoyed, is a source of strength for seasons to come. Just as the gardener's harvest stocks empty shelves that will provide nourishment through the winter, autumn intimacy feeds the heart of the relationship.

In this season, experiences of intimacy are commonplace, often undramatic. Some couples enjoy intimacy when they let all pretense fall away and engage in some childlike play: running through the woods, swinging in the park, or dowsing each other in a water fight on a hot day. Others, like Howard and Page, experience a precious moment of autumn when they first cuddle together in bed at the end of the day.

In the autumn season, the couple is present to such moments and sees beyond their ordinariness. They glimpse the mystery that is at the center of their covenant: oneness. Just as the autumn leaves and plants left in the garden slowly become one with the earth from which they sprang, the couple becomes one with each other in the intimacy of autumn. They sense, without knowing how, that they are one with their Creator.

PRAYER

*I*n autumn, the efforts of previous seasons come to fruition. Seeds, planted in spring and nurtured through summer, mature and yield a harvest. A handful of seeds becomes food to last through the winter. Leaves, golden buds in the spring and deep green foliage in the summer, sprinkle byways and hills with brilliant color. Shortly thereafter, the leaves fall to nourish next year's growth. Autumn's bounty, flowing from months of work, seems to burst forth suddenly, delighting and amazing the gardener.

A couple's autumn prayer is much the same. Evolving slowly, it becomes a part of their way of life together. In fact, their prayer becomes so natural that, like the gardener, they are delighted and amazed when they experience God's active participation in their marriage.

Through the other seasons, the couple goes about the ordinary tasks of married life: they raise their children, go to work, and struggle to love each other completely. In the midst of it all, they try to be faithful to prayer. Sometimes that requires concentrated effort and perseverance in the face of endless interruptions. At other times, prayer is left alone to grow as it might. Sometimes their spirits are willing to enter prayer but, like the apostles, they are burdened with exhaustion. Autumn prayer is different; it is sweet, quiet, and often surprising.

"What if the two on the road to Emmaus," muses one husband, "were a married couple? Scripture never really says who they are. I like to think about the two walking together through life. Jesus is with them, and they don't realize it. Suddenly, he makes himself known to them. Marriage is like that. Jesus is with us, in us, loving each of us through the other. He is part of the relationship, and most of the time we don't realize it."

Like the Emmaus experience, your autumn prayer experience will not be recognized immediately. Rather, it will remain quietly active in the pleasant peace of an unguarded moment, in loving each other freely and without self-concern, in embracing life without chronic worry. The peace and joy of those moments are indeed a resting together in God.

From the moment you confer the sacrament of matrimony upon yourselves, you acknowledge God as a partner in your relationship. From your early beginnings, God is at work with you, in you, drawing you to himself, deepening your prayer, weaving your lives and his more intricately together. As seasons in your marriage come and go, your prayer is challenged and graced, wanes and flourishes. With God's help, it matures into an autumn harvest.

THE FRUIT OF THE HARVEST

A plant draws nourishment from soil, moisture, and sunlight. Within the natural system of the plant, these three elements work together to produce fruit. The nutrients that once resided deep in the soil and the energy that radiated its way through space from the sun effect change and growth, producing for us nourishment, pleasure, and life itself. Seldom do we consider this wonder as we sink our teeth into a crisp, red apple or a slice of bread.

In the season of autumn, your prayer is like the fruit of autumn's harvest. It is the result of God's life mingling with the unique creation of your relationship and transforming it into something that gives life to you and others. Like the food you eat, your relationship grows gradually, maturing and blossoming unnoticed. Although your entire life purpose within the covenant of marriage is to let God be present through your relationship, those moments of recognizing God-with-you is a delightful surprise.

A Quiet Difference

Prayer is not just the accumulation of words said or deeds done. It is who you become as a result of your words and deeds.

Carolyn spent her summer vacation traveling with a friend through western Europe. During that time, she felt out of touch with God, unable to feel God's presence or direction in her life. She spent three months searching, praying, and journaling as she and her companion slowly wound their way from England to Italy. In a busy café in Paris, in a dance club with a couple of sailors in Germany, on a train passing fields of wheat and poppies in the Netherlands, in a small mountain town in Austria: everywhere, Carolyn's heart was hungry for a closeness with the God who seemed to elude her at every turn.

At the end of the summer, she returned to the States with

a broader experience of the world, new friends, and many memories. Her hunger for God that had followed her across the ocean and back, however, still gripped her soul.

As her friends listened to Carolyn share her summer experiences, they noticed how much more peaceful she was compared to when she left. When they commented on this quiet peace, Carolyn was surprised. How could this be? She had been haunted with hunger for months. Where was the source of this peace?

Carolyn eventually realized that her praying, journaling, and searching had made her relationship with God stronger. It had quietly and imperceptibly made a difference.

The same is true of your prayer life as a couple in a season of autumn. You work through difficult, hectic seasons, only to discover that your relationship with God has grown stronger and deeper.

Marie and Art expressed surprise at the comment a friend wrote on their anniversary card: "You are an inspiration to John and me. We love to come to your home. God shares love so generously through the two of you. Thanks."

"I can't believe we are an inspiration to anyone!" shares Marie. "We haven't done anything special. We just try to live a good life, raise good kids, and be faithful to God. We try— but I don't know how well we succeed."

This couple is a model of prayer in the autumn seasons of marriage. They are an example of what Thomas Merton refers to in his prayer called "Thoughts in Solitude": "The fact that I think I am following your will does not mean that I am actually doing so. But I believe that the desire to please you does in fact please you. And I hope I have that desire in all that I am doing. I hope that I will never do anything apart from that desire. And I know that if I do this, you will lead me by the right road though I may know nothing about it."

Marie and Art desire to please God in how they live their marriage. As their partner, God leads them along the right road. They don't know all the good that comes into the world as a result of their covenant; they know only the struggles, the shortcomings, and the hard work. They are the Emmaus couple with Christ in their midst.

"A friend of ours ministers to families and couples as a retreat master and spiritual director," shares one woman. "One day I told him about an image of heaven I had been given during my grade-school years. We are all like bottles and jars of varying size and shape. When we get to heaven, we will all be happy because each of us will be filled to the top with God. Some of us will be able to hold more because we're made larger to start with. But we will all be as happy as we can be. My friend responded, 'True, but our capacity to hold God can stretch or shrink. We can stretch our containers to hold more, or we can shrink it from disuse!'"

SOME DYING...

One way of stretching your capacity for a relationship with God is by letting go of the familiar and embracing the element of change that is part of an autumn season. Faith enables you to accept change gracefully and with hope.

An elderly woman talks about coping with an illness that keeps her at home. She and her husband playfully experience God in the midst of her limitations. "I never thought I would need to have someone bring Communion to me, that I wouldn't even be able to go to Mass. It's hard to stay home so much. I can't do much. I pray every day. I have a long list of people to pray for. I don't know what I'd do without Steve. He does the shopping, runs the errands, and puts up with me.

I'm lucky to have him. One night when I felt very sick, I sat on his lap and told him that when I go, he should marry someone else. He laughed and said that if I go, he'll start smoking up a storm and hope to join me soon. I told him it would be just his luck that he'd get himself in terrible shape and then meet someone he loved! We laughed about it. I guess he doesn't mind taking care of me. We've been through a lot together. Something good will come of this. God always gets us through."

Trusting in God's grip on your life and letting God be your strength will help you meet the other seasons of life with less inner turmoil. "When the factory laid off so many workers," remembers Julie, "we knew John's job would probably be next—and it was. But we were surprisingly calm about it. Years ago, just thinking about the possibility of him being out of work kept us up all night. This time, we prayed. For months, we prayed for wisdom to know what to do. Now that it's happened, we know God will come through. I'm working part time, and John has some interviews coming up. It's surprising; we still stay up late trying to map out our next move, but we're not frightened."

Dealing with the challenges of raising children is another area where couples experience less tension in an autumn season than at other times. "Our daughter has a learning disability," explains a young man. "There are times when her performance at school or her behavior in group situations has been traumatic for us. We yell more at each other and over-react because we're frustrated and worn out. I get moody and lose sleep trying to figure out what to do.

"But every once in a while, when our daughter is having a difficult time, we seem to slip into a space where we let go of worry and trust God. We seem to know somehow that God is part of it all and that we'll have what we need to battle this problem successfully. At those times, the lack of stress and the sense of peace are a surprising respite, like a sudden cool breeze on a muggy day."

...AND SOME RISING

Couples experiencing an autumn season are no longer struggling to hold on, to know all the answers, to chart every move. They have become attuned to God's providence. Trust has grown and they are willing to let God be God. They are ready for new life. A couple in the autumn season is able to accept change in prayer styles and practice and to develop new ways of being together with their God when the old ways lose meaning.

Being comfortable with their faith together and believing God is with them help a couple explore new ways of speaking their hearts to God and of listening to him together. This faith and hopefulness in the three-way relationship opens new horizons of prayer to the couple.

For example, perhaps one of you finds spiritual support in a Bible-sharing group, while the other doesn't. Maybe recitation of common prayers remains meaningful to one of you, while the other prefers more spontaneous prayer. In autumn, these differences are drawn together in shared moments of prayer. A monastic hour once a week, right in your living room, allows you the opportunity to pray together as a result of the spiritual growth you've realized individually. You each pray silently in your own way, but together, you are before the Lord.

Fasting together is another form of joint prayer that respects your individual prayer lives. "Even though Frank is at work and I'm at home," points out Clare, "we feel close through our prayer of fasting. Volunteering in a soup kitchen made us more aware of the poverty in our city. We feel powerless to do anything. We've decided to fast on Wednesdays. Whenever I want to eat, I offer a prayer for the poor and for people of vision to lead our country. I also think of Frank. Sharing prayer in this way is intimate for us no matter where we are."

Autumn prayer also grows out of changing situations. Newly married couples must learn to recognize and accept each other's approach to prayer. This is true in marriages where the spouses come from different denominational backgrounds as well as with couples who share similar faith traditions. In autumn seasons, the partners are less threatened by different approaches; they see their differences as a grace, a way of enriching their common prayer.

Blended families present another challenge. Second marriages experiencing autumn seasons are able to form new traditions by combining and modifying old ones, finding what is truly meaningful in both histories, and discarding trappings that are more habit than help.

WHERE IS THE SEASON?

The autumn season of prayer allows you to be more aware of God in your midst. You take time to enjoy God's presence as you are strengthened for other seasons to come. The slower pace and reflective character of autumn invite you to pray together. Time is precious. Perhaps you add an after-dinner walk to your routine. Maybe you take an unscheduled afternoon drive just to enjoy the scenery and God's splendor.

Perhaps you recognize God in your midst as you watch a daughter celebrate Communion for the first time or watch a son wait at the front of the church to meet his bride. Perhaps it is when you celebrate your twenty-fifth anniversary and remember that not too many years ago you wondered if you'd make it through fifteen. In these moments, you find the season of autumn and recognize God in your midst.

The contemplative nature of autumn invites you to reflect on how the colors of life change, how parts of life break loose and dance through the air at the mercy of time and circumstances. Whether you're married two years or sixty-two years, you reflect on the dying and letting go—and you reflect on the new life budding forth. Just as the leaves of autumn become food for next year's growth, so do your life experiences and your prayerful reflection on those experiences.

In autumn, your prayer is more contemplative. It is not so much something you *do* as something you *are.* Your prayer is a resting in God. You are always resting in God, of course, but in autumn, you are more aware of that reality—and more at peace.

Prayer in autumn is never experienced as a point of "arrival"; there is no ultimate mystical union with the holy One after which there is no more struggle. In autumn, which may be only a passing moment some busy afternoon, you are graced to rest peacefully in the Lord, knowing your covenant is embraced by the unconditional love of your third Partner.

Winter

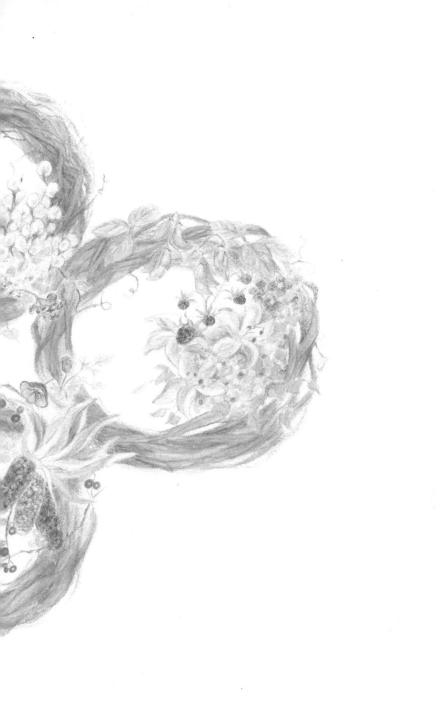

*T*he creek looks clearer during the cold months as it slides over the rocks. Not as much life is moving within to stir the silted bottom. In the woods beyond, empty branches click against themselves in the wind. Birds who have chosen to remain search for feeders or shelter among the pine branches, ready to pull seeds from open cones.

Walking back toward the house, I slip on the snow-coated grass. The earth is frozen and unyielding. Sometimes the hill is covered with deep snow. When that happens, the children appear on sleds, saucers, and skis, laughing their way down to the creek, each trying to be the one who glides the farthest.

At other times, the gray skies yield cold rain. Days are spent inside, watching the birds and the trees through the window.

Winters in a marriage force the couple inside too—inside themselves. Cold and harshness from illness, death, financial difficulties, relocation, or personal tensions within the relationship cause the couple to search their hearts for strength, for hope, for the faith to survive.

How the relationship survives depends on how deeply the couple has sunk their common and individual roots, where they will find nourishment from their love, their faith, and God. Winter is especially menacing to young plants whose roots are not well established. Close to the surface, they quickly freeze or get torn from the soil by biting winter winds. The same is true in a relationship.

Yet, harsh as they are, winters in marriage are not seasons to be avoided. They are necessary to new and deepening life, just as they are in the world of nature around us. Cold forces the life blood of plants deep into the roots so the plants not only survive but emerge in the spring, vigorous and able to grow larger and more lush than the year before. Winter has the same effect on marriage.

In a relationship, the cold can be the absence of good feelings, open communication, joy in being together. It can be the presence of anger, resentment, and barriers that put distance between the spouses. Events outside the relationship, beyond the control of the couple, can also cause winter to descend on a relationship: illnesses, deaths, hardships, agonizing over difficulties in the lives of those important to the relationship.

Whatever the cause, the cold forces the couple to retreat from normal routines and return to their roots, their center, the essence of their relationship. A couple facing winter needs to redirect time and effort that was previously going to support other endeavors (children's activities, job, community involvement, hobbies) and use it to nourish their own roots of love and commitment.

Sometimes one spouse recognizes the need first and responds individually, taking time for prayer, reflection, and solitude. Eventually, however, the couple must descend together into their common heart, their common root, to see what's wrong. What is dying? What needs to be revived? What must be allowed to die for the health of the relationship? This requires courage and faith: courage to face difficult truths, and faith that God will not let this union fall apart under the strain.

Remembering that Jesus covenanted himself to them when they covenanted themselves to each other is a crucial exercise for couples in the midst of winter. Jesus gives hope when the couple's hope runs out. Calling upon God's sacramental presence makes embracing the death and cold of winter possible and the resurrection and healing of spring a reality.

Just as nature's winter is full of breathtaking images and subtle colors and patterns that can be seen at no other time, winters in a marriage allow a couple to see beauties in their relationship that are sometimes overshadowed by the busyness and abundance of other seasons.

Winter beauties are simple:

- Rediscovering the enjoyment of conversation, even though it's painful
- Listening to each other and rediscovering each other's uniqueness
- Letting go of hurt
- Crying together
- Being on both the giving and receiving end of life
- Working together

When a winter season is used well, the couple can look forward to a sweetly intense spring. Seeing a winter season on the horizon can fill a couple with hope—not dread. They know that the throes of winter can bring the three of them—God and each other—closer than they've ever been.

Winters are not failures in a marriage any more than they are in nature. Winters are necessary for spring growth, for summer's abundance, and for autumn's harvest. Vines need trimmed, each differently.

What causes winter in a relationship, how long it will last, and how the couple survives it will be unique to each relationship. The feelings of loneliness, however, of cold and distance, will be similar. The fear and discouragement are something all married couples can relate to.

One young married couple, hearing about the winters of marriage, said, "We've only been married four months, and it's hard to believe that such times exist. But it's good to know about the winters—that they are not the end."

Winters are not the end. They can be, of course. When recognized as a winter, however, when embraced and explored, winters serve the covenant unlike any other season. Winters are beginnings.

COMMUNICATION

Winter is a time when the activity of life seems to stop, at least on the surface. In reality, however, the activity has moved to a deeper level. In the garden, deep beneath the frozen ground, life continues. Nourished by sap that has descended to escape the cold, plants live and become strong again, ready for new spring life. The environment on the surface has become hostile, so living things retreat to a deeper place where they can survive until warmth returns.

Winter in a relationship means a pulling back as well. A husband and wife may pull back *together* from life's harsh realities and demands that have put distance between them. It can also mean the pulling back *as an individual* member of the couple. When the relationship itself is the hostile environment, one partner may need to retreat into his or her own center, to seek nourishment from other places and from God before communication can again be shared freely.

Winter communication differs from the easy, constant flow

of self-revelation and sharing evident in other seasons. During these difficult times, a husband and wife must choose to communicate—and in the midst of winter, that is extremely difficult. "We were taking a long walk together," one husband volunteers. "I had a lot on my mind, but I was afraid to bring it up. I started to a couple of times but just couldn't get the words to come out. It was easier to let the silence reign. We returned home as quietly as we had set out, nothing resolved, nothing brought to the surface."

Even something simple, like saying "Good-night," can require a conscious choice when one partner feels distanced from the other. I remember listening to a couple talk about communication while my future husband and I attended a marriage-preparation program. They shared troubles they'd had communicating over the years. We just smiled at each other and held hands a little tighter. While we appreciated the presenting couple's honesty and applauded their perseverance and success in recovering from periodic breakdowns in their communication, we knew our life together would be different. We never had any difficulty talking or sharing ourselves. Poor communication? No, we knew that would not be something we had to struggle with.

Ah, such naive bliss. Before many months of married life had passed, we realized our communication was not as perfect as we had thought. Nor was it impervious to winter chill.

Amanda, married seventeen years, shares her thoughts about communication in winter seasons: "What I have become painfully aware of over the course of our marriage is that many of our fights would have never happened if we had been communicating in the first place. If Greg would have just expressed his thoughts to me and vice versa, things wouldn't have gotten misinterpreted. This was hard for me to admit to myself at first, because I always thought we had good communication skills. When I compared us to our parents, I always gave myself a pat on the back and thought how much more we discussed our feelings."

Winter communication differs from that of summer. Both can be short and utilitarian, but the couple experiencing the summer season knows that they're working in the same garden. They take reassurance from the fact that somehow they are one. Winter doesn't afford that luxury to the couple. In winter, the couple experiences a cold distance, a sense of being alone. As one woman said, "It feels like your personal concerns are of little consequence to your spouse." This is the season when hearts are most vulnerable to that whining voice that says, *You're not appreciated, not understood.* When that happens, self-pity, ego, and insecurity try to take hold of the usual love center of the relationship.

COMING IN FROM THE COLD

Winter communication differs from that of autumn. In autumn, the partners are comfortable with each other. Autumn silences are alive, flowing with reassurance and familiarity. In winter, the silences are uncomfortable, tense, and strained. They can be filled with negative thoughts and anger. Winter silences feel cold and barren. Winter communication is often sparse and unfulfilling. Because partners don't feel "received" or "held" by their spouse, they look for meaningful communication elsewhere. Struggling to get beyond these feelings and confronting the problems that have caused them is winter's great challenge.

One women shared an incident that helped both her and her husband realize how far apart they had drifted. "I was enjoying a long phone conversation with a friend. We laughed and talked about our families and our thoughts and feelings on a number of topics. After I hung up, my husband observed, 'You don't spend that much time talking with me!' I thought about that a minute and realized that, sadly, he was absolutely right. 'My friends want to be with me,' I told him. 'They want to talk. I feel an acceptance with them that I don't feel with you. I can relax talking with my friends. When you and I talk, I feel like we're always on guard.' "

Sometimes the inability to communicate comes not from a distance already present in the relationship but from some outside event like illness, a problem with a child, or the loss of a job. At these times, one or both of the spouses feel threatened or guilty and unable to honestly express their feelings. Instead, they seek friends or perhaps find a support group that helps them deal with the problem.

Colleen and Joe share their struggle with Joe's job loss: "I had been the sole income earner in our home since our marriage. I felt like I had failed. I hadn't looked for a job in twenty years. I was scared, but I felt I had to present an image of strength to my family. They depended on me. I got resentful and depressed. It was easier to talk to the other guys who had been laid off too."

Colleen continues: "I knew Joe felt horrible about it. He seemed so vulnerable that I didn't want to share my own anxiety with him. I thought he needed me to be positive and supportive. But I needed to let my feelings out, to talk to someone, so I talked with a friend who lived nearby."

Another husband remembers difficulty talking about his daughter's learning disability. "For a long time, we couldn't talk about it. I thought we needed help, but my wife wanted to work through the problem on our own. After a while, frustration and anger carried over to other areas of our life, and we weren't communicating well about anything. The school counselor referred us to a support group of other parents of children with similar problems. It helped to be able to talk to someone else."

When couples don't feel comfortable within in the relationship, they go where they feel wanted and needed; they look for "warmth" as the cold of winter slices through their marriage. Besides looking for support for a particular problem, a husband or wife may look to involvement in other areas when they don't feel at ease in their marriage. Everyone wants to feel valued, and if they are not getting affirmation from their primarily relationship, they may turn to other sources for support. Good causes are easy to find, and every church or school is happy to have a volunteer.

"I was getting so busy with 'good causes' I hardly saw my husband," shares one woman. "We passed in the morning and sometimes at dinner. Often at night one of us was already asleep when the other came to bed. It was easier than enduring silence or arguments."

How many times have you heard the off-hand comment that a good marriage is one in which the husband and wife go in different directions? "He goes his way, I go mine" is often held up as a "healthy" model for marriage. Taken literally, however, different directions create and prolong the season of winter. Avoidance becomes the norm. Granted, many couples can be involved in different careers, hobbies, or community services and find their different interests actually pull them closer together. Other couples, however, let their individual interests become a means of avoiding pressing problems within the marriage.

A danger of winter is that, on the surface, it can seem to be good, like a busy summer. The couple discusses household and financial issues, children and family, even some common interests. Mistakenly, they see this as "warmth," as a way to hold off or avoid the blast of winter. But a covenant calls a married couple to deep sharing.

MEETING THE COLD STRAIGHT ON

As difficult as winter communication can be, couples who long to experience the fullness of the other seasons will take on the struggle. They will come away from the surface "warmth" that is falsely sustaining them and meet the cold straight on. There is work to be done in winter if the relationship is to bear the rich fruit it is meant to bear.

Notice how plants sacrifice their unessential parts to endure the natural elements of winter: trees shed their leaves, for example. Couples experiencing a winter season do the same thing; they let go of the nonessentials and move to their roots, the center of their persons. They stop focusing on externals, on the little things that bother them—things that can become major blocks to communication during the winter stretches. Because it's easier to see only the negative in the harsh cold of winter, couples consciously try to look beyond the small things and talk with the person underneath. Frustrating and hurtful as this might be, it is necessary.

"I hated to bring up the issue of time spent away from home again," says Maureen. "I knew I would end up crying, and Andy would get defensive. But I felt alone and resented his involvement in so many other things. Sometimes I felt like I was raising the children on my own. I *had* to bring it up. We were getting further and further apart. I was so aware of everything about him that I didn't like. I really couldn't hold a kind thought in my head about him. I knew we had to start talking—at least a little—if we were to get through that time."

WHERE IS THE SEASON?

Communication in winter, even about little things, requires faith that Jesus is part of the relationship. Talking to your spouse when you're not sure how you'll be received requires a commitment to the covenant. You purposefully choose to try to get lines of communication open. A belief that God will give you strength and will guide your efforts to something fruitful helps you "make the first move."

During this time, when you don't feel like lovers at all, the friendship dimension of your relationship becomes crucial. Best friends help each other face difficulties because they know their friendship will deepen in the effort. Best friends encourage each other when difficulties seem insurmountable.

In marriage, your friendship will sustain you when romantic feelings are buried beneath the cold surface. You can enjoy common interests without feeling threatened. An evening walk, a game of tennis, or a good movie can begin to open lines of communication. One woman shares the joy she found in an evening spent with her husband and another couple: "We had dinner and shared good conversation. The time was lighthearted. It helped me remember other times we had like that, and I realized that we still could just go out and have fun. We still enjoyed each other's company and laughed at the same jokes. We had been so serious for so long!"

Remaining friends gradually leads to a deeper trust, to a renewed interest in each other, to a warmth that is being temporarily overshadowed. As you become aware of the qualities that drew you together, of the dreams you share and the common fears you carry, you find communication begins to flow more naturally. With God's help, you are able to listen with a warmer heart and to hold each other with a warm embrace—and the icy fingers of winter begin to melt.

FAMILY

*M*any realities can be a source of winter in family life: job, finances, children, illness, relocation. Winter-like experiences in family life can develop from difficulties within the couple's relationship as well. Whatever the source, the result is a strained, demanding period that requires strong faith and commitment to the covenant.

When the partners in a marriage are unhappy, angry, or restless, the negativity spreads to others in the family. How the couple relates to their children, their friends, their extended families, and their coworkers is influenced by the tension they experience living together and the preoccupation with their relationship that sometimes results.

One woman shares, "I didn't realize our difficulties were so obvious to the children until our fifteen-year-old daughter put her arm around me and said, 'Don't worry, Mom, it'll get better.' "

Patricia says, "I had no patience or desire to help with

projects or homework. I was always thinking about conversations I could have with Bill about what we could do to get closer again—and wondering if we ever would. Questions or needs of the children seemed like impositions, interrupting my thoughts and my ongoing internal struggle. I lost my temper with them, although the problem was really between Bill and me. I know they could feel the tension."

Winter seasons are not only the result of difficulties between a husband and a wife. Sometimes the stress of dealing with another family member brings winter cold into a couple's experience of family life.

"Nothing has caused as much strain on our relationship as our twelve-year-old daughter who thinks she's an adult," shares one father. "The final word is *weary*. I find myself truly wishing that we could just let go and trust she'll turn out fine no matter what we do—and no matter what she does. But we're not there yet. Raising a strong-willed youngster is definitely the greatest challenge I have ever faced; it's definitely the greatest strain on our marital relationship!"

Part of the winter experience in marriage stems from the different experiences and expectations the couple brings to parenting. As they look for ways to respond to their infant, toddler, young child, teenager, or adult child, the differences become more obvious. Each parent looks for solutions that align with their own experience and perception. While a couple may think they know each other, the experience of parenting will reveal new sides to them both. The challenge of winter is to work through these difficulties, blend expectations and values, and create a mutually acceptable course of action. Until that time, however, the cold winds of winter will bite at their relationship.

The teenage years offer the sharpest example of the demands a winter season makes on a marriage. Everyone has heard stories of the horrible teenage years. While they are not always so horrible—and they do bring much joy and pride as well as pain—the years when children are striving to become independent adults add tremendous tension to family life. The child who is a source of so much joy can also be a source of pain and self-doubt. Parents ask themselves over and over, "What did we do wrong?" They wonder if perhaps it wasn't so much what they did as what they didn't do. These years are times of uncertainty, when the future of their child is unknown. It is a time that demands much trust in God-with-us. This is especially true when the problems of an adolescent are serious, like drug addiction, failure in school, or chronic depression. Dealing with the guilt and struggling constantly to find answers contribute to winter seasons in family life.

THE UNCERTAINTY OF WINTER

Family difficulties that bring the bite of winter may range from minor tensions to major family crises; anything that creates uncertainty will indicate that winter lurks. Things as simple as becoming overcommitted and overscheduled, for example, can strain family life and marriage. The activities are good: sports, music lessons, dance, camp, church committees, clubs, jobs. But running from activity to activity, with no meaningful time together, will generate distance, tension, and uncertainty.

"We all seemed sullen and uncommunicative," says one mother. "I think we were all stumbling along wondering if anyone else really cared. I couldn't figure out why. We were all busy with interesting projects and activities, but we were grouchy, ready to pounce at the least thing. Then I realized that for several weeks, our schedule had been nonstop."

Illness can be another cause of winter cold. "My mother has

Alzheimer's disease," comments a mother of three young children. "It breaks my heart. Mom and I can't even carry on a simple conversation about my children. I can't share with her any of the little things the kids do: their first steps, their first days at school, the funny things they say, the interesting things they do. Mom's even afraid to eat. She can't remember what the different foods are, and she is afraid something will make her sick.

"My brothers and sisters and I all take turns caring for Mom in our homes. But when she's here, it's like having a baby in the house. She can do so little for herself. When she is staying with us, I get so down, so worn out—and I can tell that it affects the mood of the whole house."

The months following Doug's first heart attack were especially difficult for him and his wife, Sandy. They were used to hopping in the car and driving for hours to visit friends and family; after the heart attack, Sandy and Doug were afraid to go anywhere. Not wanting to be far from familiar doctors, they spent most of their time at home. Diet was changed and meals were carefully scheduled around medications. Spontaneity and enthusiasm were chased away by concern and uncertainty. Everyone noticed the difference. The grandchildren missed working with Grandpa in the shop or romping in the backyard. It took months of prayer, experimenting with medications, undergoing follow-up tests and evaluations, and learning to balance caution with a natural flair for living before the couple was able to relax and resume most of their activities.

Death of a parent puts great stress on a couple's relationship as well. "My father's death two years ago caused me to withdraw and be less open," admits one husband. "I'm not sure I've opened up yet. Maybe some, but not like before." This father of three cites the need to reestablish ties to his family of origin, the increased time and responsibility caring for his widowed mother, depression, and the differences in how he and his wife deal with their grief as some of the sources of strain on his marriage.

Sometimes a winter-like experience of family life is brought on by occurrences outside the family. Loss of job and subsequent financial stress have been common pressures for families as they try to cope with an economy in recession. Karen, for example, had chosen to stay home while her children were growing up. Recently, however, she joined the work force because her husband, Bruce, lost his job. Like so many others, his plant cut back production and laid off many longtime employees. While Bruce works part time and looks for employment, Karen works at a local restaurant. The couple manages to make it day by day but are always behind in bills. "I've been so desperate," Karen admits. "I don't know how much longer we can keep on like this. I know Bruce is trying to find work, but it's hard not to get angry. We never thought anything like this would happen to us. We just keep praying and living one day at a time."

Working two jobs, excessive traveling, and expanded responsibilities shared by a shrinking work force are other cold realities of the winter season that cause couples to struggle.

One woman expresses how discouraged her husband has become with the lack of ethics and values in his field. Her own business, once thriving, is at a standstill. "As you can tell," she says, "we feel the bleakness of winter in our jobs and that affects our marriage."

A winter brought on by outside forces can bring a couple closer together, perhaps in a flurry of summer-like activity, as they deal with the problem. At other times, however, a family winter can create a galelike force that pushes the couple apart, each retreating inside himself or herself to find a solution.

WHERE IS THE SEASON?

One temptation of a winter-like season is to insulate yourself from the elements, wrap up in anger or resentment, or bundle up in excessive activity; anything seems better than facing the hurt and disappointment of a failure. One or both of you may be unwilling to deal with a painful or difficult reality in your relationship.

"When I accepted a new job, we moved to a larger city," remembers Jake. "The job that sounded exciting and full of opportunities for creative input, though, turned out to be very disappointing. The expectations were constantly changing. I was so busy and discouraged with work and seldom took time for my family. To make things even more tense, Margaret found it difficult to get involved in the community. At home with the baby and no friends or family to talk with, she soon lost the romanticized image of the new job, new house, and new people. We were discouraged with ourselves and each other.

"At first, we didn't talk much about our feelings, but the disillusionment showed in other ways. Our conversations were pretty shallow, and we often got angry over little things."

One cannot hide from winter blasts forever. The couple committed to their covenant will accept the cold and face the barrenness together. They will cling to their third Partner and do the hard work of weathering winter, trusting in the promise of other seasons. They will experience the deep growth that comes from returning to their roots—where they will gain strength to meet the challenge of the season.

One deep winter experience in any marriage is the terminal illness of one of the partners. Accepting the reality of his wife's cancer, one husband went to his center to explore his faith. He invited his wife to share that same exploration. As they talked about God, about what they believed, about their doubts and fears—about things they had held privately most of their married life—they found hidden strength. They became constant and loving companions. Rather than retreat in silence behind closed doors, this couple bravely ventured into the elements, where they found the buds of spring. They were a source of strength to their family.

Wherever the frigid blasts come from, embracing the winter seasons as they arrive—again and again—is not easy. It takes faith. Although the cold is not dissipated, the pain is not lessened, and the uncertainty is not quieted, the couple claim the promise of sweet seasons to come.

After the widow of a Navy pilot had remarried and raised four children, she again had to face the winter of losing a husband. They were beginning to look forward to retirement together when he became ill. As they met the gauntlet of tests, chemotherapy, and waning strength, they developed a renewed sense of love and appreciation for the gifts each had to offer. They did not retreat from their feelings of anger, grief, and frustration. After her husband's death, the wife was able to pray: "Please, God, may the courage we've shared remain with me. Thank you for twenty-eight years." Meeting the suffering honestly gave the couple a chance to feel the support and love of a relationship that would be a comfort to the wife for years to come.

Winter is a cold, harsh season. But embracing it enables a couple to enjoy the coming of spring. It is faith in the coming of spring and in the active presence of God that makes embracing winters possible.

INTIMACY

When a couple experiences a winter season, the very reason for their being together seems threatened. One or both may no longer desire to share themselves deeply. One or both may no longer feel held by the other. Unlike spring, when time is never long enough for lovers to say all they want to say, to get lost in each other's arms and be together, winter is a time of feeling alone. Time together accentuates the distance, even when the two are in the same room—the same bed. For all lovers, these feelings (or lack of feelings) are frightening. The lovers find themselves wondering if the crisis will pass, if their marriage will survive.

"I remember sitting alone in the living room and crying late one night," shares one woman. "I can't remember what caused the distance we felt, but at the time, I was sure our marriage was ready to dissolve. Now, eighteen years later, I look back and smile. That was only the first of a lot of difficult times. But the pain and fear were real—and I had no one to confide in. I thought that everyone would be shocked and that we were probably the only ones to ever feel that way."

Couples who have experienced winter and the spring that follows know that the cold and loneliness of the season are no less painful—just less frightening. They know winter is only a season; it will pass. They know that the more wholeheartedly they enter into the season, the more beautiful and intense their spring will be.

Gardeners, surveying the patch of winter ground that was full of green plants and produce in other seasons, see only skeletons of last year's crop. Sometimes covered in snow and ice, the winter garden seems a dead, empty place. To a couple experiencing a winter season, their relationship seems equally dead and empty. Moments of warm encounters are memories of a time long past, memories that can fill a couple with longing and apprehension. "I would like to be alone with Keith and recapture the closeness and intimacy we once had," shares Christine, "but I'm not sure Keith wants this and that really hurts and frightens me. Have we gone too long in neglecting our relationship to ever be close again?"

This fear of failure or rejection often keeps one of the partners from taking the first step, and distance between them grows.

One woman shares how this distance showed itself in a physical way. "When we are experiencing a difficult time and feeling separated, we often end up sleeping far apart. Instead of cuddling up next to each other when we get in bed, we cling to our own little space, hanging on opposite edges of the bed. We are not close in spirit. We can't get close physically either!"

Sometimes bridging such distance seems impossible, and

the couple may be tempted to accept it as their new way of life together.

Oh, well, thought one wife, *we really aren't together on our journey anyway. I suppose I should resign myself to the fact and just get on with life.*

"I could tell something basic had changed," volunteers one husband. "We weren't arguing; we weren't upset with each other. But the sharing was not as deep. It was as if some important part of us was pulling back."

THE EFFECTS OF PULLING BACK

How or why does this "pulling back" begin? A growing sense of distance and a busy pace in other areas of life cause the marriage relationship to be neglected. Because the relationship was once strong, however, creeping winter seasons are often ignored by a couple; they assume that the chill will pass. But, like a garden left untended, the relationship will begin to suffer from the neglect; winters wreak havoc.

When you do not feel important, when you do not feel your whole personhood being held, when you feel like your spouse is not genuinely invested in your life, you will pull back. The risk of sharing deeply only to find a lack of interest coming from your spouse is too great. Pulling back protects your heart, much as a bulb nestles deep in the soil while a coat of frost settles in the garden. When couples pull back, they draw strength and comfort from their individual inner spaces or from other relationships.

Stephanie remembers a winter in her marriage: "William seemed constantly negative about his job and life in general. He wasn't communicative at all. I became lonely and tired of looking on the bleak side of things. I decided to pursue my own path, confide in my friends, and build a life that didn't exactly exclude William—but didn't depend on him either. I was determined to thrive on my own, maybe even flourish!"

Another wife remembers how she and her husband were busy with their respective careers. "We got out of the habit of sharing important stuff; we certainly didn't share our hearts. After a while, I decided to quit trying and quit hoping for a closer relationship. I kept my deep feelings to myself and went through the motions of being married."

"I had a moving religious experience while attending a meeting with some members of our parish," shares Roger. "When I tried to share my experience with Maryann, she was very negative. I think she felt threatened, since my experience was so different from hers. That happened with a few other things, too. After that, I decided to keep certain thoughts and feelings like that to myself. We couldn't share—but at least we avoided hurt and arguments."

Sometimes individuals have difficulty sharing intimately because they've gotten out of touch with themselves. The demands of life have become overwhelming, and they are no longer sure who they are or what they want. Although the sense of being out of touch could be shared with a spouse, it is often too painful and risky.

Yet, the risk has to be taken if winter is to lead to abundance in other seasons. When one partner has the courage to admit confusion or emptiness, the relationship is given a chance to step out into the brutal elements of winter, to gain strength, to prepare itself to bear fruit in another season. Those times become sacramental moments; God touches and heals the relationship and renews the covenant. Grace abounds.

REMAINING FAITHFUL

Everyone needs to feel support from outside themselves. In a marriage relationship, spouses are ideally the most significant source of support and love for each other. In the midst of a winter season, however, when the relationship between spouses is tenuous, a husband or wife may begin to look for that support elsewhere.

Sometimes that support comes from a relationship with a coworker or a friend at the local gym. It can come from the parents who share coffee in the morning after their children have left for school. It can come from the people who gather at a bar for an after-work drink or at the golf course on weekends. It can start with casual conversation and deepen when a common interest, a common concern, or a sympathetic ear is evident. Once a person who is experiencing the loneliness of winter in his or her marriage begins to feel listened to and appreciated by someone else, the temptation is to neglect the marriage. When someone starts feeling comfortable somewhere else, he or she is less likely to continue working on rejuvenating and strengthening the marriage. It is much easier and more immediately rewarding to spend time with other people.

Keeping an intimate relationship vital and growing year after year is hard work. It involves much more self-sacrifice, risk, and compassion than beginning a new friendship. Marriage is a vocation that requires every measure of love every day of your life. In seasons when love flows abundantly and easily, when its joy and comfort are evident, relating is easy. Such abundance, however, does not characterize winter. Rather, in winter, love seems frozen; one feels cold and alone. Remaining faithful to the marriage demands great faith as well as personal effort.

During those times, it's easy to forget that marriage is your vocation. No one likes to feel hurt, unloved, unlovable, or trapped. How tempting to enjoy the warmth of other friendships to the exclusion of working on the relationship at home. This is "holding back." It does not necessarily mean sexual infidelity—although that can be a danger. It means finding other people to hold a part of your person that used to be held by your spouse. Not much in our society reminds you that marriage is a covenant. When you are hurting and frustrated, it's difficult to remember this. It's like trying to remember the beautiful view when you're trudging through a snowstorm. The vista is swallowed by swirling snow; all your energy is focused on your instinct for survival.

I am reminded of an old story Robert Fulghum tells in his book *It Was on Fire When I Lay Down on It*. A visitor to the French city of Chartres comes to see the great cathedral being built there. He talks to workers as they leave for the day and asks what they do. One replies that he is a stone mason and spends his days carving rock. Another says he blows colored glass for windows. The last, a sooty blacksmith, replies that he pounds metal all day long. The visitor then enters the dark building and sees a woman busily sweeping up piles of wood shavings and bits of rock and glass. When asked what she is doing, she replies without hesitation, "I am building a great cathedral for the glory of God almighty!"

That was a person of vision. Her job was small, but she knew she was part of a great work. Winters in marriage are a time to remember that you, like the lady sweeping debris in the partially constructed cathedral, are building a cathedral for the glory of God almighty. Your covenant is a place of worship and prayer. It is a sign to the world, like a cathedral, that God loves us all and is present in the midst of this world. It is difficult to remember this when you're hurting, lonely, and discouraged. But you are not alone. God is a partner in the covenant.

Of course, not all "outside" support is a potential source of problems for the marriage. A couple needs friends; no one person meets all the intimacy and social needs of another. Other friendships and involvements, provided they respect the sacred reality of the covenant, enrich a marriage. Especially in winter, these "others" can support the couple as they struggle to "keep warm." These friends can remind the couple that winter, like other seasons, serves its purpose and then gives way to life.

"When I felt really discouraged about my marriage, I talked with my friend down the street," remembers Carla, married ten years. "I could share my fears and feelings, and she would listen. I knew she respected Brian and me, and I didn't feel like I was being unfaithful by turning to her for support. She was a great help when I needed someone to listen. She and her husband had been married longer than we'd been, and she shared some of her stories. I really took heart listening to her."

PHYSICAL INTIMACY

When a person does not feel held on an emotional, intellectual, or spiritual level, sharing intimately on a physical level can be difficult. One is reluctant to become vulnerable when he or she has been hurt or is feeling unimportant.

Physical intimacy is a sign of oneness, of the desire for unity with the other, the whole other: mind, spirit, and body. Physical intimacy is an expression of the deep sharing that already exists on other levels of the relationship. When sharing on other levels is absent or limited, the act of physical union can actually heighten the couple's sense of loneliness, of their lack of union in other areas. It can deepen the distance, making one feel used or desired for only one part of who they are.

However, the act of making love can also be a sacrament, a deep encounter with each other and with the compassionate God whose love they share. At those times, making love can break through barriers and help begin a process of healing. The willingness to risk, to be vulnerable again, opens the couple to God's working deep in their hearts.

"I remember crying after we made love," confides Nancy. "Tom asked me what was wrong—and I didn't know. I just knew that I hurt and that so many feelings seemed to pour out of me. We were finally able to talk. I told him how bad I felt about our relationship and that I was afraid. It was the beginning of communication again for us."

Sometimes physical intimacy is affected by other circumstances beyond the control of the couple. Prolonged illness, depression, or experience of sexual abuse earlier in life can affect a couple's physical intimacy. One woman shared their experience with infertility and the strain it placed on their relationship.

"The springtime of hope for starting a family for us turned into a bleak and tortuous winter. Having always seen myself as a wife and a mother, the prospect of childlessness rocked my self-esteem and identity to the core. Our communication broke down. Intimacy became regulated by the thermometer and calendar and lost most of its joy and spontaneity. It took years to find the spring again."

Believing that God is part of the commitment, even if you don't feel it, gives you a sense of support and strength. You're able to move forward, one day at a time, through the sometimes long and bleak winters of marriage.

"Looking through my journals, I noticed that I often asked God to help us get through our difficult times," says one woman. "But just as often, I would ask if God was with us at all. Always, though, I ended with a short prayer for help. I guess I always believed, deep down, even though I doubted."

WHERE IS THE SEASON?

Faith gives you the courage to face winter seasons head on. One husband, married sixteen years, shares this reflection on winter: "The challenge of winter is to enter into the season and come out into the cold. Rather than remain locked into ourselves, introspective, withdrawn, uncommunicative, we need to open up to each other and share the pain, share our woundedness."

When you experience a winter in your intimate sharing, the most difficult task is to take the first step into the cold, to admit to each other the difficulty, and to face it together. Not to embrace the season and recognize the things around you that are painful and need "pruning" is to remain alone.

"What happens to make intimacy difficult?" asks one husband. "Familiarity and responsibility. What gives strength to keep trying? The alternative of not sharing and being within one's own world in which communication continually diminishes."

Loving each other is a conscious choice, not a feeling. Although this is a phrase often heard on retreats for married couples, nowhere is it more significant than in the winters of your marriage. Embracing the season is to embrace the cross, as Jesus did. Choosing to love often means choosing to die to self. It is what makes true intimacy possible.

Intimacy helps you get through winters in other areas of

your lives as well. "I had surgery, possible breast cancer," shares Irene. "Intimacy with Jack gave me strength and comfort. From the security of his arms, I could see that so many others suffer tremendous loneliness and uncertainty."

How this intimacy is shared will differ from marriage to marriage. "It's like those children's books that let you decide how the story will progress," explains Irene. "If you want the characters to choose one course of action, you are instructed to 'turn to page such and such.' If you want the characters to choose a different course of action, you are instructed to turn to a different page." Of course, you don't choose the "adventures" life gives you, but you do choose—with or without God's help and with or without the benefit of your spouse's involvement—what the adventure will mean to you in terms of growth.

"Successful marriages seem to be the ones that 'talk' through experiences," shares one husband. "Eskimos spend the many long hours of winter retelling their stories. That's important. They reaffirm who they are through those stories. Married couples need to spend the time of winter sharing their story."

Remembering is part of the warmth of winter.

"We'd talk and argue and get angry with each other," remembers one husband. "But, even during the times when it took weeks or months to work through something, we would remind ourselves that we'd been through these times before and made it. We'd remember some of our successes, some of the good times. It helped us keep at it and not give up."

Couples who refuse to give up take the risk of facing the cold together. They ask, cry, and seek warmth where their covenant is respected. Embracing the winter in their intimacy, the couple trusts in the harvest of seasons to come.

PRAYER

*P*rayer is a natural part of a covenant, a constant thread that varies according to the season. It may be formal and structured, free and spontaneous, intense and serious, light and playful. For those living the covenant of marriage, prayer is always living in relationship with love. Mother Teresa says, "Do small things with great love." That is the challenge of married life and the source of much prayer.

Sometimes a couple's prayer flows naturally and spontaneously. Whether the partners pray together or by themselves, their beloved is in their heart and is brought before God in their prayer. Woman and man as wife and husband are covenanted to each other and God—and God to them. Thus, prayer is not only words spoken; prayer is choice, discernment, action, and rest. A couple who is close to each other and to God is a prayer just in their being. The three-in-one relationship offers praise to the Creator. It carries the presence of the holy One into the marketplace, the neighborhood, the world. Because the relationship is a large part of prayer in marriage, prayer suffers when winter hits.

Prayer as a relationship with God is subject to the same obstacles that trouble the relationship: a busy schedule, a low priority, being taken for granted, becoming routine and superficial.

When a marriage is venturing through the hazards of winter, God seems distant and uninvolved. Jesus' prayer becomes the couple's prayer: "My God, my God, why have you forsaken me?" Situations outside their life together and problems within the relationship can throw a couple's prayer into the cold grasp of winter.

Unable to sense God's presence with them in their covenant, the couple may feel abandoned or wonder if God was ever with them in the first place. "Maybe God didn't play as big a role in our coming together as we've been thinking all along" is a common lament when winter settles in a marriage.

Deana and Justin have been married five years. "Justin and I seemed to be drifting apart. We didn't talk much about anything important. I didn't look forward to seeing him at the end of the day like I once did. Our relationship felt cold and empty. *Maybe we were wrong,* I thought. We had been so sure that God had brought us together and that our marriage was a response to God's call. I remembered something we had heard in our marriage-preparation course, that love was not just something you felt but a choice you make. I was having a hard time choosing love, and I didn't feel God's help. It was a scary feeling, thinking we were in this alone."

Another couple experienced this same "scary feeling" when their miracle didn't materialize. The wife's cancer was inoperable. Once, while having lunch with the husband, I offered my prayers.

His response reflects the cold depths of despair that winter can bring. "We are past hoping for miracles," he said. "We've prayed and prayed. I don't know what else to do." His face was filled with pain and exhaustion.

Losing the sense of marriage as primarily a spiritual journey is part of the frozen tundra in the season of winter. Prayer loses its priority. "We could never find a good time for prayer," says one mother of young children. "We just couldn't fit it into the schedule. When we left it for bedtime, we always fell asleep." Her husband echoes her thoughts: "It's easier to ask God to wait than the boss who expects the report handed in tomorrow. I know that isn't the way we should order our life. We try, but I'm afraid we aren't very successful. When we exchanged our marriage vows, the spiritual dimension of marriage was important to us. But what was central early in our relationship easily gets pushed behind other concerns and activities. When that happens, our relationship suffers. Prayer becomes difficult."

TWO PATHS OF PRAYER

One husband reflects on how he and his wife experienced their faith from two different vantage points. "When I was enthusiastic about getting more involved in our parish, Lynn had little enthusiasm. She halfheartedly supported my attempts. When I tried to share some insight or something that had been meaningful to me, she listened, but I didn't feel like she really heard me or was happy for me. When I asked her about that, she apologized and explained that she felt her own prayer life was weak, almost nonexistent. She didn't mind my involvement, but her lack of support or interest made it difficult for me to continue."

One partner's doubt (sometimes a reaction to a loss or

crisis) can bring doubt into the other's faith or into the relationship itself.

Being in different places in their individual prayer journeys can affect how well a couple shares prayer. It also affects closeness in other areas.

"We had not been married very long when we discovered our experiences with and understanding of Scripture were very different. Early attempts at Bible-sharing were disastrous," recalls one couple.

A married person retains an individual prayer life, an individual relationship with God, as well as entering into a new joint relationship when he or she marries. Each partner's prayer can, as we have seen, affect the other. While one cannot abandon his or her personal path to step into the path of another, the two can be a great support by remaining faithful and sharing their individual experiences.

How can a couple experience God when winter haunts their relationship? How can they experience prayer when one or both feel distant from God?

THE PRAYER OF PRESENCE

Once, the superior of a religious community told me about their custom of praying when someone in the community was having a particularly difficult time. At night, while the troubled Sister slept, the other Sisters would gather in the chapel and spend hours in prayer for her. She might never know of her community's special support, but the strong, intense prayer made a difference. The same can be true in a marriage relationship.

"More things are wrought by prayer than we can imagine," explains the English poet Alfred Lord Tennyson.

Roseann shares her experience of such support when she was feeling the need to get back in touch with God. She was afraid; she felt like her past sins and neglect of God had left her abandoned in the eyes of God. "I wanted to talk to a priest, but I was so nervous. Then, Gus offered to go with me, to sit in church and pray for me while I met with the priest. His support and prayer made all the difference. I know I never would have been able to go through with it without him."

Another couple talked about times when they were having problems in their marriage. The wife doubted God's help in getting through the rough times. Her husband, however, clung to faith, believing that God had been with them from the beginning and would remain faithful. "When I saw how much Dale believed that God was with us," says Terry, "it helped rekindle my own faith. It put hope back into my heart."

The support of prayer for one's spouse is especially supportive during times of separation. One woman, soon to celebrate her fiftieth wedding anniversary, shared a prayer she wrote and prayed each morning while her husband served overseas during the Second World War: "I got down on my knees and prayed this every morning: 'Dear God, hear this prayer right from my heart. Take care of Joe while we're apart. Guide him when he's far away and bring him back to me some day.' I still say that prayer today for Joe."

Other people can offer support for the couple as they struggle through a winter in their prayer life. "So many times I relied on other's prayers," says a mother whose two daughters had serious medical problems. "Sometimes I just couldn't pray. One day I would be on my knees praying nonstop, and other times I couldn't pray at all." Knowing that a close friend, a member of your family, or a spiritual director is praying for you and believing in you helps you keep faith.

Couples' prayer groups or Bible-sharing groups can also be a source of spiritual support. In a small group, as the level of trust grows, the sharing deepens. Couples feel freer to ask for prayers. They receive encouragement as others share stories of their own struggles and perseverance.

THE PRAYER OF TEARS

In the midst of a winter season, a couple's prayer may be tears. Physically and emotionally worn out by the struggle, whatever it might be, words fail. Alone, or clinging to each other, they both cry.

Tears can be an eloquent prayer, pouring out feelings, hopes, and fears too deep for words. Father Edward Hays, in his book *Pray All Ways,* speaks of the prayer of tears: "He was touched by the sorrow of the widow who was on her way to bury her only son. 'Do not cry,' he restored her son to life. His heart was deeply touched, and without any request from the mother, he performed a wonder, a miracle. Her tears were her prayers, and those prayers were heard. Tears are indeed powerful prayers, for they possess the power to move even heaven. Tears perform numerous functions besides being the most powerful of all languages. Tears are able to express that which is beyond the power of words."

The young couple whose two-year-old daughter had been battling a rare cancerlike disease said they were on a complete roller-coaster ride of emotions. Trying to stay on an even keel was difficult but important for them and their daughter.

"We went from hearing bad news and fearing the worst to receiving good news and getting our hopes up higher than we should," remembers the wife. "Then, about six months after our daughter's diagnosis, I gave birth to our second daughter, Elizabeth. We were thrilled. News of Maggie's illness had gotten around, and our parish priest came to visit me at the hospital—to see the baby and offer support. He gave me a little finger rosary.

"The next morning my doctor came in and said that he'd heard a little murmur in the baby's heart. He wanted to send her to be checked by specialists. I was shocked. I'm sure I didn't hear everything he told me. I just nodded my head and went along with it all.

"Elizabeth wasn't in any immediate danger, but she was all hooked up to monitors, little wires, and tubes. Before they transported her to a hospital where specialists would check her, the staff took a picture of her for me. When I looked at my little Elizabeth, all wires and monitors, the tears really came. I couldn't pray any words. I just held on to the finger rosary Father Tom had given me and I cried."

Saint Paul could be speaking of the prayer of tears when he says that when we do not know what to say, the Spirit intercedes and prays for us in a way that cannot be put into words. "The one who searches hearts knows what is the intention of the Spirit, because it intercedes for the holy ones according to God's will."

THE PRAYER OF SILENCE

Silence, too, is a powerful prayer. Worn out and cried out, their anger or frustration spent, the couple can do nothing but sit in silence before God. Perhaps God will speak in that silence; perhaps all they will hear is silence. Yet, to place themselves before God is an act of faith; it is prayer.

When they moved from a rural setting to Chicago, one

couple had a difficult time adjusting to their new surroundings; their relationship experienced a lot of stress. Although they had shared prayer many times, the cold winds of winter kept them uncomfortable with any form of joint prayer. "We decided to sit together for a half an hour each morning in silence," remembers the husband. "In our own way, with our own silent words, we brought our pain and confusion to God. Although we didn't say anything together or do anything together—except sit—we were still able to find comfort knowing we were sharing prayer the best we could."

"Be still, and know that I am God" is a prayer that can comfort a struggling couple. When you're unable to understand the meaning of your life together, to bring some kind of order into the chaos and see where your life together is taking you, remember that there is One who knows and who will not forget you. You are called, like Samuel, to come before your God and listen.

In the book *New Seeds of Contemplation,* Thomas Merton spoke of the temptation to despair when we cannot feel the presence of God with us: "Place no hope in the feeling of assurance, in spiritual comfort. You may well have to get along without this....Faith must be deep enough to subsist when we are weak, when we are sick, when our self-confidence is gone, when our self-respect is gone. I do not mean that faith *only* functions when we are otherwise in a state of collapse. But true faith must be able to go on even when everything else is taken away from us."

Although Merton's words are not addressed to married couples, they are as true for a couple's joint spiritual journey as they are for an individual's journey. Broken hearts are often humble hearts. Recognizing their own creatureliness, the couple is receptive to the holy One. They have nothing else on which to depend.

WHERE IS THE SEASON?

When a couple faces a crisis, their prayer is often more intense, more frequent. Faith can be the one point of stability in otherwise tumultuous times. One couple married thirty-eight years recalls such faith and prayer: "Two of our children almost died. God was present in each of these situations. We prayed on the way to the hospital each time, and we felt peaceful that God was in control, and he was."

That sense of peace is not always present, especially when what the couple hopes for does not come to pass or the outcome of a situation is difficult to accept. Sometimes it seems that prayer is falling on deaf ears—if it's falling on ears at all.

As in any other facet of married life, the challenge of prayer in the winter of marriage is to enter the season. This can be particularly difficult, since feeling distance from God in the relationship and questioning the reality of God's participation in the covenant leave you feeling very much alone.

As in an individual's journey toward God, however, be willing to enter the cold desolation of winter. Only there will you experience the warmth and joys of spring. In fact, winter prayer may be your most earnest prayer. How much easier to sit down and talk to the Lord or trust God in your relationship when your life together is going well, when your family is healthy, your job secure, your love strong. Even "going through the motions" is easier when life, while not without it's problems, is not falling apart. True winter prayer is authentic, rising from hearts that are empty, broken, or filled with sorrow.

"We used to pray for certain things: for something in our children's lives or for restored health," shares an older woman who deals with a chronic illness. "Now we pray 'Thy will be done,' and trust that God knows what is best for us. It isn't easy, though."

Lady Julian of Norwich wrote: "He said not 'Thou shalt not be troubled, thou shalt not be travailed, thou shalt not be distressed,' but he said 'Thou shalt not be overcome.' It is God's will that we take heed to these words, that we may be ever mighty in faithful trust in weal and woe."

Embrace the season of winter with hope—even when hope seems lost forever. One couple shares their experience of a long deep winter that touched all aspects of their life together. They struggled to keep the relationship alive: they sought counseling and forced themselves to keep trying, although they seemed unable to endure the stress and pain it had caused them both. They needed all the faith they had—and more—to walk through the season. The wife shares these thoughts as she looks back over the years: "Winters are never easy, but we have seen the impossible happen. We have seen a relationship in shambles become the joy of our lives and a source of strength. I still don't like winters while I'm in them, but I don't fear them anymore, and I have great hope and trust in the sacrament and in our third Partner."

A strong, faith-filled marriage is a powerful presence of God in the world where the elements of evil are very real. Couples who try to remain faithful, who desire to respond to God as a third Partner in their relationship, should not be surprised that their prayer will be challenged. It is challenged by many aspects of our times and culture. It is challenged by life-draining forces that entangle the covenant. Yet, faithful to the covenant, God is present always, sustaining the relationship. Whatever season you are experiencing in the moment, your covenant is a sign of hope, faith, and God's presence, for yourself, for each other, and for the world.